MW00789704

"In *Pastoral Care and Intellectual Disa* pastoral theologians to participate in the 'dream work and soul work' of imagining a prophetic and creative church: a church in which disabled people are supported and encouraged in their calls to ministry. The book is a valuable addition to conversations about pastoral imagination and the arts of relationships that contribute to human flourishing."

—REBECCA F. SPURRIER, *Associate Dean for Worship Life and Assistant Professor of Worship, Columbia Theological Seminary*

"Anna Katherine Shurley points the Church toward postures and practices that enable people with developmental disabilities to flourish in caring communities, and she invites these communities to flourish as well because everyone belongs."

—ERIK CARTER, *Cornelius Vanderbilt Professor of Special Education, Vanderbilt University*

"*Pastoral Care and Intellectual Disability* advocates for typical relationships with persons with intellectual disabilities. The person-focused approach to these mutually beneficial relationships, particularly between pastors and persons with disabilities, makes the book unique and radically countercultural."

—JEFF MCNAIR, *Professor of Education and Director of the M.A. in Disability Studies, California Baptist University*

"Proclaiming that 'all Christians are called to give care to and receive care from one another as a reflection of who they are as the Body of Christ,' Anna Katherine Shurley summons people with and without intellectual disability to faithful discipleship and mutual care. Anyone seeking to welcome people with and without disabilities into Christian life together would benefit from reading this wise, joyful, and practical book."

—WARREN KINGHORN, *Associate Research Professor of Psychiatry and Pastoral and Moral Theology, Duke University Medical Center and Duke Divinity School*

SRTD
STUDIES IN RELIGION, THEOLOGY, AND DISABILITY

SERIES EDITORS

Sarah J. Melcher
Xavier University, Cincinnati, Ohio

and

Amos Yong
Fuller Theological Seminary, Pasadena, California

Pastoral Care and Intellectual Disability

A Person-Centered Approach

Anna Katherine Shurley

BAYLOR UNIVERSITY PRESS

Cover design by Rebecca Lown
Cover image: Illustration by George Wilson, courtesy of the artist and Creative Growth Art Center

Library of Congress Cataloging-in-Publication Data

Names: Shurley, Anna Katherine Ellerman, author.
Title: Pastoral care and intellectual disability : a person-centered approach / Anna Katherine Shurley.
Description: Waco, Texas : Baylor University Press, [2017] | Series: Studies in religion, theology, and disability | Includes bibliographical references and index.
Identifiers: LCCN 2016058523 (print) | LCCN 2017026554 (ebook) | ISBN 9781481307369 (ebook-Mobi/Kindle) | ISBN 9781481307352 (ePub) | ISBN 9781481301701 (web PDF) | ISBN 9781481301695 (pbk.)
Subjects: LCSH: Church work with people with mental disabilities. | People with mental disabilities.
Classification: LCC BV4461 (ebook) | LCC BV4461.S55 2017 (print) | DDC 259/.42—dc23
LC record available at https://lccn.loc.gov/2016058523

Series Introduction

Studies in Religion, Theology, and Disability brings newly established and emerging scholars together to explore issues at the intersection of religion, theology, and disability. The series editors encourage theoretical engagement with secular disability studies while supporting the reexamination of established religious doctrine and practice. The series fosters research that takes account of the voices of people with disabilities and the voices of their family and friends.

The volumes in the series address issues and concerns of the global religious studies/theological studies academy. Authors come from a variety of religious traditions with diverse perspectives to reflect on the intersection of the study of religion/theology and the human experience of disability. This series is intentional about seeking out and publishing books that engage with disability in dialogue with Jewish, Christian, Buddhist, or other religious and philosophical perspectives.

Themes explored include religious life, ethics, doctrine, proclamation, liturgical practices, physical space, spirituality, and the interpretation of sacred texts through the lens of disability. Authors in the series are aware of conversation in the field of disability studies and bring that discussion to bear methodologically and theoretically in their analyses at the intersection of religion and disability.

Studies in Religion, Theology, and Disability reflects the following developments in the field: First, the emergence of disability studies as an interdisciplinary endeavor that has had an impact on theological studies, broadly defined. More and more scholars are deploying

disability perspectives in their work, and this applies also to those
working in the theological academy. Second, there is a growing need
for critical reflection on disability in world religions. While books
from a Christian standpoint have dominated the discussion at the
interface of religion and disability so far, Jewish, Muslim, Buddhist,
and Hindu scholars, among those from other religious traditions, have
begun to resource their own religious traditions to rethink disability
in the twenty-first century. Third, passage of the Americans with Disabilities Act in the United States has raised the consciousness of the
general public about the importance of critical reflection on disability
in religious communities. General and intelligent lay readers are look-
ing for scholarly discussions of religion and disability as these bring
together and address two of the most important existential aspects
of human lives. Fourth, the work of activists in the disability rights
movement has mandated fresh critical reflection by religious prac-
titioners and theologians. Persons with disabilities remain the most
disaffected group from religious organizations. Fifth, government
representatives in several countries have prioritized the greater social
inclusion of persons with disabilities. Disability policy often proceeds
based on core cultural and worldview assumptions that are religiously
informed. Work at the interface of religion and disability thus could
have much broader purchase—that is, in social, economic, political,
and legal domains.

Under the general topic of thoughtful reflection on the religious
understanding of disability, Studies in Religion, Theology, and Disability includes shorter crisply argued volumes that articulate a bold
vision within a field; longer scholarly monographs, more fully developed and meticulously documented, with the same goal of engaging
wider conversations; textbooks that provide a state of the discussion
at this intersection and chart constructive ways forward; and select
edited volumes that achieve one or more of the preceding goals.

Contents

Acknowledgments   ix

Introduction   1

1   Collaborating   11
    A Person-Centered Approach to Pastoral Care

2   Empowering   27
    The Psychological Architecture of Person-Centered Pastoral Care

3   Calling   45
    The Theology of Person-Centered Pastoral Care

4   Playing   61
    Person-Centered Pastoral Care in Practice

5   Witnessing   87
    Person-Centered Pastoral Care and the Church

Notes   107

Bibliography   135

Index   145

Acknowledgments

Just as it takes a village to raise a child, it takes a village to write a book. I have been blessed with an extraordinary village of people who have loved and prayed me through this project—a village that spans several states, congregations, neighborhoods, and institutions.

I am grateful to the staff and clients at a particular center for children and adults with developmental disabilities who, for several years, gave me the privilege of serving as their chaplain and friend. I cannot share their identities, but they know who they are. They shared their lives with me and showed me the extraordinary things that God can do in and through people with intellectual disabilities. My years with them were some of the most rewarding of my life. Their wisdom and friendship undergird every word of this book.

The Reverend Bill Gaventa first introduced me to the fields of disability studies, supports, and theology during my doctoral studies at Princeton Theological Seminary. His enthusiasm was contagious—so much so that I chose to write a dissertation on pastoral care and disability. I am grateful for his friendship, his guidance, and his tireless advocacy for people with disabilities. Along with Bill Gaventa, Amos Yong and Sarah Melcher saw this book's potential for inclusion in the Studies in Religion, Theology, and Disability at Baylor University Press. I am thankful to them—not only for advocating for my book, but also for shaping my thinking about the intersection of faith and disability through their own gifted writing. Carey Newman and Emily Brower at Baylor University Press guided me through the editorial process with patience and humor. Their careful attention to the details of my work, along with their commitment to this project, has been bread for my journey.

I could not have spent the concentrated hours necessary to write this book had it not been for friends and family in Radford, Virginia; Titusville, New Jersey; Monroe, Louisiana; and Gulfport, Mississippi, who took time out of their days (and sometimes weeks) to take care of my children. Their love for our family and their belief in the importance of this project sustained me during my writing and helped me remain faithful to the many different components of my own vocation. This mother, wife, minister, and academic is indeed grateful.

My parents, Kay and Gary Ellerman, have long believed that my brother and I could do anything we set our minds to. In addition to nurturing our gifts and strengths, they have shown us, by their own examples, how to follow Jesus with our whole heart and mind. They have taught their children well, as I hope this project will attest.

My husband, Will, has been a constant source of strength and encouragement since my earliest days of doctoral studies and dissertation writing. Our partnership as spouses, parents, and ministers is quite a gift, and I could not have written this book without it—or him. He tells people that in marrying me he got the long end of this deal. I beg to differ.

Finally, I want to thank my precious children, Virginia and Oliver. I have been working on this project as long as I have been their mother. I pray that they will never underestimate their ability to be faithful to God's call—even if and when God calls them to do big things. I dedicate this book to them with all my love and joy.

"Now to him who by the power at work within us is able to accomplish abundantly far more than all we can ask or imagine, to him be glory in the church and in Christ Jesus to all generations, forever and ever" (Ephesians 3:20-21).

—Anna Katherine Shurley

Introduction

God wants all of God's children to take good care of each other. God's desire is not simply a gentle invitation: it is a directive, a summons, a call. No one is exempt from God's call—even God's people with intellectual disabilities are called to be caregivers. Intellectual disability does not nullify a person's call from God to care for his or her brothers or sisters in Christ, nor does it diminish his or her capacity to do so. In and through their common life, all Christians are called to give care to and receive care from one another as a reflection of who they are as the body of Christ. As the Apostle Paul writes in his first letter to the Corinthians, God has carefully crafted the body of Christ such that "the members may have the same care for one another" (1 Corinthians 12:25).

Christ's body on earth is at its best when all the various kinds of individual minds and bodies within it can work together and care together as God intended. In the body of Christ, no member is more capable or self-sufficient than another; every member of Christ's body needs every other member to flourish so that the body can be truly whole. No matter how strong some members of the body might be, they cannot be at their strongest unless all other members are functioning as they should. If any one member of Christ's body is compromised, the whole body suffers. Members of Christ's body need one another and depend on one another, just as Jesus and his disciples needed and depended on one another during his time on earth. As the perfect Son of God, Jesus could have accomplished the tasks of his earthly ministry without the help of humans, and certainly his gracious work of redemption was something only he could under-take. Nevertheless, Jesus abandoned a position of power to become a servant—a caregiver—for those whom he alone would ultimately redeem, and he invited others to join him in his work.

Jesus' ministry healed and restored individuals and communities. He healed lepers and demoniacs who were forced to live apart from their communities because of their debilitating conditions. With a simple touch and a concise command, Jesus restored wholeness to broken bodies and minds and enabled them to be welcomed back into the communities from which they had been estranged. Jesus also healed the broken spirits of tax collectors, adulterous women, and other sinners whose communities had shunned them for their bad choices. Through prophetic words shared in the context of simple acts of friendship and hospitality, Jesus loved people into healthier and more faithful ways of living that would no longer alienate them from others. Jesus' healing and caring acts of ministry enabled individuals and communities to be whole again and empowered them to live new lives according to his most perfect Way.

Jesus was the ultimate caregiver, yet he also welcomed care from others. He let a devoted woman anoint his feet with expensive perfume; he enjoyed meals served by hospitable friends; he welcomed the hugs and kisses of children who sought to show love to him. Jesus did not only welcome the care and love of others; he needed it. On the night of his arrest, Jesus asked his friends to stay awake with him and pray as he anticipated his death. Jesus needed his friends; he needed their care. Similarly, Jesus also knew that his friends needed one another, and he called them to care for one another as he had cared for them. He instructed his disciples to wash one another's feet just as he had washed their feet. He reminded them that they would be recognized as his disciples by their love for one another. From the cross he asked his mother and his beloved disciple to move forward from his crucifixion as mother and son, caring for each other as family. In his own life and death, Jesus demonstrated the deeply communal nature of the kingdom of God.

By assuming a posture of servanthood and friendship in his earthly ministry, Jesus demonstrated that life in the kingdom of God is, fundamentally, life together. Then and now, Jesus asks people to follow him together—to choose community in their care for one another and in their life of faithfulness. At its best, life together in the body of Christ is life that imitates Jesus: a life marked by mutuality and servanthood. Once again, the Apostle Paul explains it clearly in his directive to the Philippian church: "Let the same mind be in you that was in Christ Jesus" (Philippians 2:5). Christians are called to have the mind of Christ, a servant who did not seek power but who, instead, sought out fellow servants and friends for shared community and ministry. Jesus calls people in all times and places to follow his examples of mutuality and care, because, as his own earthly ministry proved, God never intended God's children to live life any other way.

Jesus' ministry sets the terms by which his people should continue his work today. For Jesus, ministry involved partnership with all kinds of people with different kinds of gifts and abilities. His initial group of twelve disciples included fishermen, tax collectors, and zealots. Eventually, he would count women and former Pharisees among his followers. In spite of their differences—or, perhaps, precisely because of them—Jesus and his followers were able to accomplish far more than they would have without a diversity of kingdom workers offering whatever they had to their Lord. The church needs a diversity of witnesses to carry out Christ's ongoing work on earth. As Paul writes in 1 Corinthians 12, the church needs people whose minds and bodies work differently so that the world can experience the love and grace of God in different ways. Because of the need for a multiplicity of expressions of God's good news, members of the body of Christ need to embrace people of all abilities and disabilities as fellow servants and fellow caregivers, thereby modeling for the world the love and friendship of the Christ who first loved and befriended them.

The Christian community cannot flourish unless all its members can actively participate in Christ's ministry of servanthood and mutual practices of care—including its members with intellectual disabilities. An essential task of the church is to proclaim, in word and deed, that Jesus died and rose to reconcile all people to God and to one another, despite the differences—including disabilities—that might otherwise divide them. Without the contributions of people with intellectual disabilities, faith communities present to the world a diluted, incomplete proclamation of the scope of Christ's redemptive work. In and through Christ and by the power of the Holy Spirit, all bodies and minds can have abundant lives in which they offer important acts of ministry to their communities. The world will only know that this good news is true if and when it sees the good news in action. For this reason, Christ's church needs people of all abilities and disabilities to share God's love and care with one another in ways that reflect the friendship and love of Christ himself.

Achieving this kind of robust witness is really not an impossible feat. The very same God who breathes life into every human being equips every human being with the ability to live out his or her purpose. Since God calls all people to take good care of one another, God enables human beings with even the most profound intellectual disabilities to participate in the practices of care to which they have been called. Likewise, God enables typically functioning people to embrace their brothers and sisters with disabilities as the friends and fellow servants that they are. God's Holy Spirit is alive and at work in every human life, empowering every human mind truly to have the same mind that was in Christ Jesus by serving others and being served and by caring for others and receiving care.

Unfortunately, the norms of society do not reflect the mind of Christ. Despite God's active working in and through every human mind, there are minds outside Christ's body who doubt that people with intellectual disabilities can flourish. In fact, some of the world's minds do not even believe that people with intellectual disabilities should be allowed to be born. Contemporary perspectives on intellectual disability, as well as societal stigmas and misconceptions about the lives of people with intellectual disabilities, threaten not only the health and wholeness of Christ's body but also its witness to the world. Inspired by Enlightenment thinker Francis Bacon, who believed that no disease should be considered incurable and that all medical knowledge should work toward the prolongation of human life, many geneticists and champions of genetic research believe that disability can and should be alleviated altogether.[1] Their belief is based on the assumption that disability is a disease that fills life with suffering and misery. In their opinion disability should be eliminated or, better yet, prevented.[2] Indeed, genetic testing often reduces disability to something that people can choose to avoid. Through genetic testing, prospective parents can calculate the risks and benefits of trying to conceive a child by determining whether or not they are carriers of genetic disorders that cause disabilities.[3] In prenatal tests such as amniocentesis, doctors test developing fetuses for genetic variations—primarily Down syndrome—allowing expectant parents to choose whether to proceed with the pregnancy or to terminate it. In fact, the majority of abortions that occur after amniocentesis are a response to a diagnosis of Down syndrome, even though contemporary medical advances can enable people with Down syndrome to live long and fulfilling lives.[4] Since the option to terminate a "genetically defective" pregnancy is available, parents who choose to bring into the world a child with Down syndrome or other intellectual disabilities risk judgment from the medical community and from a society that cannot understand why anyone would make such a choice.[5] Similarly, many expectant mothers (particularly those of advanced maternal age who have a statistically higher likelihood of having a baby with intellectual disabilities) often feel pressured by their doctors to undergo prenatal genetic testing so that they will have the option to terminate a pregnancy if disability is discovered.[6] Any couple's decision to give birth to children with disabilities seems absurd in the wake of centuries of scientific thought and progress aimed at strengthening the human race.

In a sense, contemporary innovations in genetic technology are simply more sophisticated versions of the eugenic practices of the late nineteenth and early twentieth centuries that endeavored to tidy up the human race by preventing the birth of unfavorable children—including those with disabilities.[7] Like the eugenics movement, genetic testing done for the sake of avoiding the birth of children with intellectual disabilities reflects society's suspicion that the lives of people with intellectual disabilities cannot be of any real and lasting value to anyone.

A pathological perspective on disability is a threat to any community. When people are reduced to the disabilities within their minds and bodies, they become an "other"; they become deviations from what is "normal."[8] Designations of otherness or abnormality breed misunderstanding or, worse, fear. With narrow notions of normality informing perspectives on disability, people living with intellectual disabilities are more readily perceived as fundamentally flawed and as proprietors of lives fraught with suffering and sadness.[9]

This kind of perspective on disability robs people with intellectual disabilities of opportunities to make a difference in their cities and neighborhoods—as well as in their faith communities.

Without carefully and prayerfully navigating these ethically challenging issues surrounding disability, the church could become society's unwitting accomplice in perpetuating negative attitudes about people with intellectual disabilities—those who are already living and those who are yet to be. If and when faith communities buy into society's perception that disability is an aspect of a person's life from which he or she needs healing in order to flourish, people with disabilities may be continually relegated to the role of care recipient in the life of the community. The shadow that this perspective casts on people with intellectual disabilities compromises the possibility of their enjoying active participation in the ministries of their congregations. Furthermore, when people with disabilities are simply seen as objects of pity in need of healing, they may be excluded from participation in the mutually caring friendships with brothers and sisters in Christ that God intends. If faith communities can only see disability as something to be eliminated, they threaten the very practices of care, servanthood, and friendship to which people of all abilities and disabilities have been called. In some respects, faith communities' complicity in societal misconceptions about disability is an honest and, perhaps, even compassionate mistake. Congregations may think it unreasonable to invite people with disabilities to be caregivers when their daily challenges and need for care appear to be so profound. Even well-meaning exclusion, though, feeds into the common myths that "normal" life and participation in faith communities require typically functioning bodies and minds.

Make no mistake: the church has not, by any means, completely failed in its ministries for people with intellectual disabilities. Whether through visitation in institutions or group homes, specialized Christian education programs or worship services, or simply inclusion on congregational prayer lists, many faith communities have offered intentional and meaningful care to people with disabilities. Every act of care offered on behalf of someone with a disability is a valuable gesture that bears witness to God's great love for all people. Furthermore, people with intellectual disabilities and their families do face unique and often profound challenges that need and deserve particular attention. Faith communities are right to address the struggles that people with disabilities endure, including complications with housing, medical care, employment, and other aspects of life. Likewise, faith communities and other pastoral caregivers are right to attend carefully to the feelings of grief and loss that people with intellectual disabilities may occasionally feel. After all, God does not ignore the struggles of God's people, and God is no stranger to the vulnerability that is at the center of all human life, particularly the lives of people with intellectual disabilities. However, since contemporary society's perspectives on disability are so problematic and harmful to people with disabilities and their families, the church and its congregations must convey a decidedly different, prophetic message about lives shaped by intellectual disability. Faith communities seeking to share God's love in ways that bear witness to the extraordinary countercultural life and work of Jesus need to be intentional about embracing people with intellectual disabilities as something more than simply care recipients. Just as Jesus welcomed unique individuals as partners in his own ministry, so too should faith communities welcome people with intellectual disabilities as co-laborers for the kingdom of God and fellow caretakers of God's people.

The culture's narrow notions of "normal" simply do not work in a community of people called to have the mind of Christ. There is nothing "normal" about the church. In fact, in and through the incarnation of Christ, God calls God's people to a way of life together that is anything but what the world calls "normal," "typical," or even "rational." After all, there is nothing "normal" about a messiah who comes all the way down from heaven and, instead of claiming the power and prominence he deserves, claims the life of a servant and gives his life for his friends. If the Christian community is to have the same mind that was in Christ Jesus, it must adopt a different kind of normal in its practices of care. The church's normal includes the recognition that people with disabilities are not problems to be solved but are gifts, just as all its members are gifts. A faith community that is "normal" according to the standards of Christ recognizes that God is both present and active in the lives of people with disabilities and is calling and equipping them to do important work for God's kingdom.

Now is the time for Christian faith communities to consider a new approach to pastoral care with people with intellectual disabilities—an approach that bears witness to the very different brand of "normal" that characterizes Christ's church. In and through Jesus Christ, Christians of all bodies and minds can live life differently and care for one another in ways that run counter to the ways of the world. By the power of the Holy Spirit, all bodies and minds are able to care for one another with the love of Jesus, regardless of the disabilities that may shape those bodies and minds. In and through a different kind of normal, the church can bear witness to God's radical love, hospitality, and friendship.

Thanks to forward-thinking experts in the field of disability services, Christian faith communities have access to resources that can help them cultivate practices of pastoral care in which people of all abilities and disabilities can actively participate. The past two decades have brought remarkable innovations in the supports offered to people with intellectual disabilities—innovations marked by the kind of creativity and partnership that the church's caring ministry needs. These secular person-centered approaches to support hinge on the belief that people with intellectual disabilities have dreams for their lives and the capacity to realize these dreams through proactive collaboration with others. Viewed from a theological perspective, people with disabilities (like their typically functioning counterparts) have vocations—particular, God-given plans for a meaningful life—that they can discover and enact in meaningful ways.

Just as people with disabilities can work with their support system in a secular, person-centered environment to give shape to their lives, brothers and sisters in Christ can work together as partners in care to help each other embrace their vocations—God's desires for their lives—disability notwithstanding. The Christian community can bear witness to God's different kind of normal by embracing an approach to pastoral care that is distinctly and intentionally "person-centered." In a person-centered pastoral care, all members of a faith community empower one another to live the lives God has created them to live. Indeed, person-centered pastoral care points to the radically counter-cultural way of life that the body of Christ is called to embrace in its life together and, particularly, in its practices of care. Advocacy for person-centered pastoral care is an invitation for the body of Christ to amplify the witness of every part of the body—not simply those that function according to the world's criteria for normality.[10] Through shared practices of care in person-centered pastoral relationships, people with disabilities can share their gifts and themselves with their brothers and sisters in Christ and do their part to keep Christ's body strong.

God calls God's people to care for one another, and to empower one another to be the people that God created them to be. God calls God's people to have the mind of Christ. If ever there was a time for the church and its members to bear witness to the countercultural gospel of Jesus, it is now. The world is fraught with distrust, division, and angry rhetoric, not to mention human interactions that are often more virtual than incarnational. Discord, fear, or even something as seemingly innocuous as technological advances can separate people from one another, causing them to lose a sense of belonging and purpose. This same kind of loss happens when stigmas surrounding intellectual disability separate people with intellectual disabilities from their communities and, especially, from faith communities. The body of Christ cannot flourish if any part of it atrophies. Unfortunately, though, atrophy is inevitable whenever people with intellectual disabilities are not able to participate fully in the body's life and work. There are people with intellectual disabilities who wonder if and to whom they belong, and if and for what purpose they matter. The body of Christ can answer these questions in and through loving hospitality and inclusive, collaborative practices of care. People with intellectual disabilities need to see and hear God's call to friendship in and through authentic, mutually caring relationships with one another. Through collaborative practices of pastoral care, the body of Christ can bear witness to the good news that all bodies and minds belong to the God who loves them.

SUGGESTIONS FOR FURTHER READING

Dollar, Ellen Painter. *No Easy Choice: Disability, Parenthood, and Faith in an Age of Advanced Reproduction.* Louisville, Ky.: Westminster John Knox, 2012.

Eiesland, Nancy. *The Disabled God: Toward a Liberatory Theology of Disability*. Nashville: Abingdon, 1994.

Hall, Amy Laura. *Conceiving Parenthood: American Protestantism and the Spirit of Reproduction*. Grand Rapids: Eerdmans, 2008.

Reinders, Hans. *The Future of the Disabled in Liberal Society: An Ethical Analysis*. South Bend, Ind.: University of Notre Dame Press, 2000.

Swinton, John, and Brian Brock, eds. *Theology, Disability and the New Genetics: Why Science Needs the Church*. New York: T&T Clark, 2007.

1

Collaborating
A Person-Centered Approach to Pastoral Care

Person-centered support is an exercise in collaborative dreaming, a true dialogue between one imagination and another. In person-centered support, a caregiver and care receiver explore the care receiver's hopes and dreams with the goal of finding ways for a care receiver to live out these dreams. Imagination fuels a person-centered collaboration; it is the means by which the partners in care consider new and different ways of living. After all, the imagination exists in all human beings and influences all thinking, feeling, and sensing, whether or not a person can acknowledge its creative activity.[1] No human life is beyond the imagination's grasp—not even lives shaped by intellectual disability.[2] Given the opportunity, people with intellectual disabilities can put their imaginations to work as active participants in practices of support and care. Not only can they make valuable contributions to their own journeys toward well-being and wholeness, but they can also make valuable contributions toward the well-being and wholeness of others. Indeed, people with intellectual disabilities can be true partners in support and in care—not simply recipients of it. By paying careful attention to hopes and dreams, partners in person-centered support may be able to transform the ways that people with intellectual disabilities live their lives.[3]

When dreams find their way into practices of pastoral care, the care becomes a means of fostering healing and growth in the lives of people with and without intellectual disabilities. As a tool in practices of care, the imagination can be an agent of God's healing—a catalyst for God's transforming work. As God's people work together to imagine lives shaped by the upside-down narrative of God and God's kingdom, they may discover the present and the future into which God intends God's children to live—as the body of Christ and as its individual members. In other words, person-centered pastoral care can help all of God's people discover and embrace the dreams that God has for them.

THE BIRTH OF PERSON-CENTERED SUPPORT

Person-centered support owes its origins to faithful dreamers in the field of disability services who have long believed that people with intellectual disabilities are more than simply passive recipients of goods, services, or care. In the late 1960s and early 1970s, people with disabilities and their advocates became increasingly critical of disability services in the United States, many of which failed to consider the personal needs and wishes of their clients.[4] Often warehoused in institutions and mistreated, people with intellectual disabilities were forced to settle for whatever resources were available to them. Disability services shaped by institutionalization, mistreatment, and ambivalence prevented people with intellectual disabilities from participating in community life—including spiritual and religious practices—and left them seeing themselves as more of a burden than a blessing.[5] Thankfully, disability advocates like Wolf Wolfensberger noticed this all-too-prevalent "wound of life-wasting" among people with intellectual disabilities. Wolfensberger and his colleagues in the United States and in Europe used their expertise in developmental disabilities to rethink how society can and should care for its vulnerable members. Concurrent with a growing awareness of the need for change in disability services came the establishment, in 1966, of the President's Committee on Mental Retardation. The committee's 1969 report, titled *Changing Patterns in Residential Services for the Mentally Retarded*, was the collaborative effort of Wolfensberger and other radical like-minded disability experts from around the world. The report brought national and international attention to the inadequacy of services for people with intellectual disabilities, and demonstrated the possibility of providing them with better, more comprehensive services and opportunities for a meaningful life.[6] Swedish committee member Bengt Nirje's contribution to the report constituted the first written account of the "principle of normalization."

This principle was the primary underpinning of a then recently established Swedish law governing care and services for the country's citizens with disabilities. Put simply, the normalization principle included provisions for making available to people with disabilities the same sorts of opportunities that are afforded to typically functioning members of society, including respect for their individual choices and wishes.[7]

In 1972 Wolf Wolfensberger published *Normalization*, an American adaptation of Sweden's normalization program. Wolfensberger's text proposes a system of disability support that helps individuals establish and maintain culturally normative behaviors and practices.[8] Despite the implications of its name, the goal of normalization is not to try to make people with disabilities fit into a prescribed social and cultural mold for the sake of fitting in or appearing "normal." In fact, Wolfensberger, aware of the misunderstanding that the term "normalization" evoked, eventually adopted a different name for his approach that more accurately reflected his commitment to affirming the value of people with disabilities as well as their roles in society. "Social role valorization," as it continues to be known, seeks to enable and empower people with disabilities to participate in society and enjoy as many experiences and learning opportunities as possible, including meaningful relationships with others.[9]

Social role valorization became a catalyst for positive change in disability supports, paving the way for collaborative practices of support and care. In 1973 social role valorization inspired the development of a series of workshops for leaders in the disabilities field. Known as Program Analysis of Service Systems (PASS), these workshops allowed participants to evaluate existing institutions and services for people with disabilities, using the principles of social role valorization as their guide.[10] Through PASS workshops, participants discovered that people with disabilities were not being treated as individuals with worth and potential; their needs, values, and gifts were often dismissed or ignored by the programs and institutions that purported to offer them quality services and care.[11] The discrepancy between services offered and the quality of life of the clients served inspired disability service providers to begin planning and providing services that not only honor their clients' particular needs but also intentionally strive to meet these needs.[12] This new way of supporting people with disabilities became known as person-centered planning and support.

The development of person-centered disability supports has enriched the lives of people with intellectual disabilities, as well as the communities in which they live. Twelve approaches to person-centered support were developed between 1979 and 1992. While each approach is unique, several guiding principles are common to all. All person-centered support focuses on the person being served, as opposed to his or her diagnostic label. Similarly, all approaches to person-centered support employ common language and images rather than professional jargon. After all, people with disabilities are not their disabilities, nor are their disabilities simply problems to be solved or illnesses to be cured. Person-centered support honors the person and also honors the fact that all people need a community in order to flourish. Each approach to person-centered support involves careful listening not only to the person being served but also to those who know the person best. Both the person being served and their "circle of support" are essential to the process of evaluating the person's current circumstances and working toward positive life changes. Individuals cannot enjoy full, meaningful lives apart from their communities. Likewise, a community cannot thrive without contributions from all its individual members. All approaches to person-centered support involve an active assessment of a person's gifts and capabilities and a search for ways that a person can make use of their assets within their community life.[13] Indeed, everyone benefits from person-centered support: individuals are able to name their gifts and find ways to use them, and communities are strengthened by the contributions of members who may have been previously overlooked.

Person-centered support uncovers a person's gifts and abilities by using what is known as "capacity thinking." Rather than focusing on a person's deficiencies, which can alienate the person from his or her community, capacity thinking begins by considering a person's gifts, strengths, and potential.[14] By emphasizing the inherent giftedness of each individual, as well as the valuable contribution he or she can make in communities when given the chance to do so, person-centered support can alleviate, if not eliminate, negative attitudes about people with intellectual disabilities. Person-centered support builds bridges where there were once barriers. In person-centered support, individuals once considered powerless, passive recipients of services (and pity), are empowered to name their hopes and dreams, and to realize these hopes and dreams within the context of life in their communities. Furthermore, person-centered support disables the dangerous distinctions between "us" (people without intellectual disabilities) and "them" (people with intellectual disabilities)—distinctions that perpetuate exclusion and compromise the possibility of authentic community.[15] Through the creative, collaborative work inherent in person-centered support, lives that might once have been wasted are empowered to flourish.

A MATTER OF VOCATION

Person-centered support is both dream work and soul work. It is an inherently spiritual activity in which caregivers and care receivers tend to the deepest needs and desires of the care receiver's soul.[16] Among these needs and desires may be a quest for life's meaning and purpose, as well as a sense of personal worth and value. Viewed through a lens of faith, person-centered support does more than facilitate community participation and contribution for people with intellectual disabilities. Person-centered support gives people with intellectual disabilities the potential to be the people that God has created then to be, and to do what God has created them to do. God has endowed every human life with a vocation—a unique and carefully crafted purpose—that needs to be discovered and activated for the good of the individual and the strengthening of his or her community. People with intellectual disabilities have particular gifts to share and contributions to make to their communities, all of which are part and parcel of their unique, God-given vocations.[17] When person-centered thinking shapes pastoral care, then, the care becomes a means of energizing the care receiver's vocation.

A person-centered quest for vocation includes attention to every aspect of a care receiver's life, since God has carefully crafted all aspects of every life for God's glory. Truly, vocation is all-encompassing; it includes socioeconomic status, habits, and location in a family and community, as well as internal qualities such as talents, interests, and attitudes.[18] Accordingly, every vocation is as unique as the person to whom it is given. God has carefully and intentionally designed every human life, endowing it with particular qualities and capabilities, all of which are essential to and intended for use in the building up of God's kingdom.[19]

God gives vocations and calls God's children to live out the vocations they have been given. All of God's children are called by God to do as much as possible with their gifts and interests—and with good reason. While the shape of vocation differs from one person to another, the crucial function of vocation is common to all: God has called all people to be witnesses, through their particular vocations, to God's work in Jesus Christ. The calling to bear witness to Christ is not contingent upon a person's feeling worthy or capable of living out his or her vocation. God has already affirmed each person's worth and capability.[20] The task of all people—including people with intellectual disabilities—is simply to proclaim the gospel with their whole being.[21]

Since everyone has a unique and important vocation, it is important to remember that vocation does not only refer to a profession or work. A person's vocation may certainly include a particular job, but the job never exhausts the vocation. In an age in which a person's usefulness and worth are often measured in terms of productivity, the idea that vocation might be distinct from work is difficult to grasp. Work, though, cannot define a life, or a calling. God calls all people—not just those who have a job.[22] To be sure, many people with intellectual disabilities are employed in a variety of settings and derive a great deal of satisfaction and fulfillment from their work. Many others, however, are not capable of having a job, nor will they ever be. Yet they, too, have a vocation. They, too, have been called by God to be witnesses in very particular ways that are unique to and compatible with their gifts and strengths.

Clarity about vocation can be healing for people with disabilities, particularly if they have never been able to see themselves as a part of God's good creation or participants in God's ongoing work in the world. Pastoral caregivers, who are agents of God's healing work, foster healing and growth in the lives of people with intellectual disabilities. Care receivers who may have once perceived their lives as having little or no value can discover in and through a person-centered collaboration just how precious and essential they really are. When a caregiver partners with a care receiver in a creative, collaborative exploration of the care receiver's interests and gifts, as well as his or her hopes and dreams, the caregiver can empower the care receiver to see more clearly that he or she has a role to play in the drama of building God's kingdom. In the ministry of person-centered pastoral care, healing and growth are the means by which people with disabilities are empowered to live into their vocations as servants of God.

While a pastoral care partnership can be a source of healing and growth as a care receiver seeks to uncover his or her vocation, the concepts of health and healing warrant careful attention when used in the context of disability. The constitution of the World Health Organization (WHO) begins by defining health as "a state of complete physical, mental, and social well-being and not merely the absence of disease or infirmity."[23] While the WHO definition of health has not changed in the nearly sixty years since its adoption, the adequacy of the definition's language is worth questioning, particularly in light of the realities of physical and intellectual disability. If achieving health is contingent upon complete physical and mental well-being, then many people with disabilities can never be healthy, since many physical and intellectual disabilities cannot be eliminated without eliminating the person living with the disabilities.[24] Health must be understood as something other than the absence of disability, and healing as something other than the elimination of impairments. For people of faith who understand their lives to be gifts from God, health most certainly has a thicker meaning. Health is a robust wholeness marked by the strength and determination to live into the fullness of God-given humanity, even in the face of challenges.[25] Health, then, is akin to the Hebrew concept of *shalom*, a wholeness of being in which a person is living the gift of life that God has given and is doing so in communion with God and neighbor. Shalom, like life itself, is a gift from God, and is found when people and communities are living as God intends for them to live.[26] If health is shalom, then healing is the restoration of shalom. Healing is the recovery of wholeness, the restoration of community, and the reclamation of the strength to live fully into the life that God has given. Undoubtedly, the challenges that come with disability can compromise a person's resolve to be healthy. Even so, disability does not eliminate the possibility of healing. Pastoral caregivers

can nurture healing in the lives of people with disabilities by journey-
ing with them toward a discovery or rediscovery of their strength to
live abundant lives of faithfulness to God. Through person-centered
pastoral care, people with disabilities can find shalom where it may
have once been lost and, in so doing, discover their vocations—God's
great dreams for their lives.

THE IMPORTANCE OF PERSON-CENTERED
PASTORAL CARE FOR THE CHURCH

Since person-centered support can help people with intellectual disabilities discover the unique vocations to which they have been called, a
person-centered approach to pastoral care holds great promise for chaplains, pastors, and Christian laypeople whose vocational commitments
include nurturing disciples of Christ—including disciples with intellectual disabilities. Pastoral care shaped by person-centered ideas can offer
hope and opportunity to individuals who may not realize how precious
they are to their Creator and how essential their gifts and talents are
to the well-being of their communities. The church and the individual
faith communities that it comprises need to cultivate and care for their
disciples so that each one can claim and live into the vocations to which
God has called them.

To be sure, many faith communities are already engaging in
intentional practices of care with and for people with intellectual disabilities and their families. Some faith communities, for example, have
chosen to develop ministries exclusively for people with disabilities.[27]
In these formal programs of care, congregations may make regular
visits to local group homes, offer camping opportunities for children
with disabilities, or establish Sunday school classes specifically for people with disabilities. One congregation, for example, once sponsored
a "Special Class Day" to bring together members of the congregation
and the people with disabilities. Their goal was to cultivate awareness
within the congregation in an effort to break down barriers between
people with and without disabilities.[28] Practices of intentional care
for people with disabilities make a positive difference in the lives of
people with disabilities and strengthen the witness of congregations.
Furthermore, ministries designed exclusively for people with intellectual disabilities acknowledge the need for faith communities to share

God's good news in ways that are accessible to all people. Nevertheless, the group-specific nature of the ministry may inadvertently leave
people with disabilities occupying positions in the faith community
that are somewhat separate—or "special." People with intellectual
disabilities do not always want special treatment. Instead, they want
to participate in the life and work of the faith community just like all
their other brothers and sisters in Christ. Undoubtedly, practices of
care designed exclusively for people with disabilities testify to a faith
community's willingness to pay close and careful attention to the spiritual needs of people with disabilities.[29] A faith community needs to be
aware of the often-unique needs of people with disabilities and their
families, just as it should be aware of the unique needs of each of its
members. The challenge, though, is for a faith community to embrace
people with disabilities as partners in a community of caregivers that
includes all people.

Embracing people with disabilities through collaborative care is
a central feature of the supportive care group model of pastoral care
with people with intellectual disabilities. This model emerged both as
a response to the increasingly complex (and often increasingly limited)
nature of medical care and human services and as an acknowledgment
of the church's historical role in caring for the needs of those within
and beyond its membership.[30] In a supportive care group, no one person assumes sole responsibility for attending to a care receiver's needs.
Instead, each member of the group participates in caregiving.[31] This
corporate approach to care presents concrete opportunities for people with and without disabilities to engage in caring relationships and
thus fosters a spirit of hospitality within the congregation as a whole.

A supportive care group can be initiated by a family member
(or someone acting on their behalf) or by a member of the congregation. The group is organized according to the particular needs of
the specific person receiving care, with the care receiver (identified as
the "dependent person") situated at the heart of the group.[32] Groups
may consist of people occupying a number of different roles, including
friends, court-appointed guardians, financial and medical advocates,
record keepers, and a spiritual mentor, whose primary responsibility
is to facilitate the person's integration into the life of the community.[33]
While much of a care group's work occurs within the context of the

congregation, the group may also collaborate with secular service providers to strengthen the person's overall level of support. For example, a supportive care group might partner with social workers, medical personnel, and other secular service providers to assist a person with a disability in making a transition from living in his or her family's home to another type of living arrangement.[34]

Supportive care groups offer members of congregations the opportunity to share their gifts with others and participate in important ministry, and at the same time they try to empower people with disabilities to do the same within the faith community.[35] While supportive care groups bear witness to the need for members of Christ's body to care for one another in intentional concrete ways, they function mostly as a caregiving mechanism "for" people with disabilities and not as a practice of caring "with" people with disabilities. People with intellectual disabilities are called to both give and receive care. Supportive care groups can provide invaluable assistance both to congregations who seek to be a hospitable space for people with disabilities and to people with disabilities who desire to be active participants in faith communities and who have specific needs that a congregation can meet. However, faith communities should strengthen their welcome even more by inviting people with intellectual disabilities to truly share in the sacred practice of caregiving as partners and friends who both give care to and receive care from their brothers and sisters in Christ.

When people with disabilities are always perceived as care receivers or are otherwise set apart in ways that limit their contribution, faith communities may unintentionally compromise the potential for people with disabilities to participate in the friendships and interdependence to which all of God's children are called.[36] People with intellectual disabilities need to be welcomed as partners in their faith communities' work and witness. It is only through true partnership that people with disabilities can experience full inclusion in Christ's church. True partnership in ministry with people with intellectual disabilities requires faith communities to be willing to abandon practices that segregate or alienate members of the body of Christ and instead to adopt practices in which all people are encouraged to participate.[37] People of all abilities and disabilities can indeed partner together in practices of care that are truly "co-creative"; authentic, meaningful care does not necessarily require sophisticated intellectual engagement. For example, pastoral care partners might communicate with one another through art or listen to music together that evokes thoughts, feelings, or emotions that they can share with one another and, in so doing, reflect for one another the love and presence of God.[38] The body of Christ, which by design consists of a variety of gifts under the same Spirit, needs a variety of voices that bear witness to the love and care of God in Jesus Christ and enhance the whole body's understand of itself and its witness.[39] When pastoral care is shaped by mutuality and partnership, the witness of people with disabilities can be seen and heard more fully, and the people themselves can be more fully recognized as invaluable members of the body of Christ.[40]

Pastoral care with people with disabilities is at its strongest when it happens in the context of authentic relationships marked by mutuality and reciprocity in practices of care. In a person-centered approach to pastoral care, all of God's people—including those with intellectual disabilities—are both caregivers and care receivers. When all members of faith communities engage practices of pastoral care as partners—as friends—they become agents of God's healing and empower one another to live into the particular vocations God has given them. Herein lies the promise of a person-centered approach to pastoral care.

HOW PERSON-CENTERED CARE BECOMES PASTORAL

While person-centered pastoral care addresses many of the same issues as therapeutic disciplines or other forms of disability support, it is nevertheless distinct in that it is a ministry of Christ's church and a manifestation of God's ongoing work in the world.[41] Whether person-centered pastoral care takes place in local congregations or in institutions or group homes, the mission and work of the church is always its context and God's self-revelation in and through Jesus Christ is always its controlling center. The ecclesiological and christological commitments undergirding person-centered pastoral care necessarily shape the ways in which caregivers employ the interdisciplinary resources that the care requires. A ministry shaped by the life, death, and resurrection of Christ takes seriously the belief that creation cannot be understood apart from the Christ event. God's revelation in Christ is the context within which all nature is examined and understood and the context within which the insights and resources of the natural and human sciences are engaged.[42]

Since God's revelation in Christ sets the terms by which all creation is to be understood, the very person of Christ can set the terms by which person-centered pastoral caregivers engage theological and social scientific resources in their ministry. A particularly helpful interpretive tool for person-centered pastoral caregivers is known as the "Chalcedonian pattern," because it is derived from the ancient church's description of the divine and human natures of Christ.[43] Drawn from the Council of Chalcedon's description of the divine and human natures of Christ, the Chalcedonian pattern describes the relationship between Christ's two natures as being one of unity, differentiation, and order.[44] When utilized in the context of person-centered pastoral care, the Chalcedonian pattern serves as a conceptual framework within which to interpret the spiritual and psychological material that emerges in the course of the caring relationship.[45] The pattern also illustrates the ways in which person-centered pastoral care is both related to and distinct from secular person-centered care. In person-centered pastoral care, a caregiver and care receiver explore aspects of the care receiver's life in which theological issues are intertwined with psychological, social, and emotional issues. Even so, psychological, social, and emotional concepts and issues cannot be translated in theological terms, nor can theological concepts and issues be translated psychologically. Finally, theological and psychological concepts and issues are related to one another asymmetrically. Theoretically, theology exists at a more comprehensive conceptual level than psychology. Theology is not, by any means, a more important discipline than psychology; rather, theology has a broader scope of inquiry. Theology addresses ultimate questions about God, humanity, and the world—questions that cannot be addressed with the resources of psychology or other social scientific disciplines.[46] Theology addresses knowledge of and faith in God that, by definition, functions at a different conceptual level than psychology. Therefore, in the context of person-centered pastoral care, the psychological issues and concerns of the care receiver are interpreted within the broader framework of the ultimate beliefs about human meaning and purpose that can be addressed only by theology.

A Chalcedonian approach to interdisciplinary thinking and ministry reflects well the theological and social scientific commitments inherent in person-centered pastoral care. Pastoral caregivers necessarily attend to both the psychosocial and spiritual needs of those in their care. At the same time, they must also acknowledge that psychosocial and theological inquiries take place within the context of pastoral care as a ministry of the church grounded in the life, death, and resurrection of Christ. Thus, practices of person-centered pastoral care bear witness to the Christ after whom all ministries are, literally, patterned.

Every moment of person-centered pastoral care is the product of a creative collaboration between a caregiver and a care receiver.[47] Pastoral care is an art, the shape of which is contingent upon the artists (caregiver and care receiver) and their unique partnership. The caregiver journeys alongside the care receiver, carefully and prayerfully listening to and exploring joys, sorrows, needs, hopes, and dreams. In this collaborative art, both caregiver and care receiver trust in the healing presence of the Holy Spirit and seek the Spirit's healing guidance as they discern ways to move forward in life and in their God-given vocations. Like pastoral care, person-centered support is more of an art than a technique. Facilitators listen carefully to clients' dreams and nightmares. They then work with their clients to shape the clients' hopes and visions into sustainable images that can be transformed into new daily routines that move clients closer toward their dreams. Person-centered support is a collaborative endeavor in which facilitators do not assume a position of power over their clients but rather work from a position of power *with* them in a process of enriching the clients' lives.[48]

The marriage of person-centered support and pastoral care with people with intellectual disabilities is the joining together of art with art, as caregivers and care receivers creatively explore their needs and dreams within the context of the vocation to which God has called them. In a caregiver's work with people with intellectual disabilities, person-centered language, ideas, and support are inevitably commingled with the spiritual reflection, guidance, and pastoral support that fuel pastoral care. Caregivers listen to care receivers' hopes and dreams and validate their ability to make choices about what matters in their lives, as well as their ability to make contributions to the communities in which they live. At the same time, whether explicitly or implicitly, caregivers affirm care receivers' worth in the sight of God and acknowledge that they too, in fact, have a vocation into which God wants them to live. While person-centered support and vocation-minded pastoral care coexist and commingle, they are nevertheless two different types of support. Person-centered support involves a community of people listening to a person's desires and dreams and working together to actualize those desires and dreams. While the ministry of pastoral care certainly involves deep listening to the needs, hopes, and dreams of those seeking care, pastoral caregivers and care receivers seek to discern the will of God, who alone is the source of healing and guidance in the shaping of lives.

When person-centered support and pastoral care come together in the ministry of the church, the goals of person-centered support are placed within the theological framework undergirding the ministry of pastoral care. In concrete terms, person-centered pastoral care is literally situated within a holy friendship patterned after the relationships between the persons of the Trinity, as well as God's relationship with God's children, made known in and through Jesus Christ. In person-centered pastoral care, a caregiver and care receiver partner together to explore and name the care receiver's dreams for his or her life and consider the ways in which these dreams can be actualized. After all, God gives each person the freedom to dream dreams and make choices about how he or she might live them out. Even so, a person's freedom to actualize his or her dreams must be understood as existing within the larger framework of *God's* carefully crafted dreams for him or her.[49] As Jeremiah 29:11 confirms, God's dreams for God's children include a future with hope, a future and dreams that are undoubtedly far more fulfilling than anything that anyone could imagine. When a pastoral caregiver and a care receiver partner together to consider the care receiver's life—including dreams and hopes—they do so in a spirit of openness and attentiveness to God's dreams for that life. After all, it is in God's dreams that every person's true self is ultimately found.[50]

The creative, holy work that transpires in person-centered pastoral care reflects a shared awareness of God's dream work in every human life. Creative, holy, person-centered pastoral care also bears witness to every human being's fundamental need to play—to dream—in a safe space with an encouraging, trustworthy playmate. The safe space of a person-centered pastoral care relationship can enable a person's true self to find expression and pave the way for more authentic living. In the context of life in and vocation from God, the pastoral care relationship becomes a sacred space in which God's nurturing, healing Holy Spirit can transform lives.

SUGGESTIONS FOR FURTHER READING

Block, Jennie Weiss. *Copious Hosting: A Theology of Access for People with Disabilities*. New York: Continuum, 2002.

O'Brien, John, and Connie Lyle O'Brien, eds. *A Little Book about Person-Centered Planning*. Toronto: Inclusion Press, 1998.

Race, David, ed. *Leadership and Change in Human Services: Selected Readings from Wolf Wolfensberger*. London: Routledge, 2003.

2

Empowering
*The Psychological Architecture of Person-Centered
Pastoral Care*

Person-centered pastoral care is grounded in the belief that healing and
growth are possible when people can play freely in their own spaces.
Everyone needs space in which they can rest, relax, and be fully and
authentically themselves. One person's space might be a specific physical location where he or she will not be bothered. Another person's
space might be a more figurative entity: a sacred moment of time when,
in solitude or in the company of friends, he or she can engage his or
her thoughts and ideas without judgment or criticism from people who
may think differently. People with intellectual disabilities need space to
dream. They need the freedom to explore and share their dreams and
their nightmares, and they need the resources with which to transform
the essence of their dreams into reality.

Like anyone else, people with intellectual disabilities also need
people who will honor their dreams and support their efforts to see
the dreams come to fruition. Even so, people with disabilities do not
always have their dreams or nightmares acknowledged. Well-meaning
caregivers often, and perhaps even unwittingly, give primacy to their
own dreams and ideas for their care receivers' lives. As a result, people
with disabilities can find themselves bereft of any opportunity to envision, much less realize, lives lived on their own terms. Just as support
providers in institutions, day programs, group homes, and even in private homes can unintentionally stifle the dreams and opportunities of
their clients, so too can churches stifle the dreams and desires of their
members with disabilities. When a faith community fails to partner

willingly with all its members in practices of care and discernment, it compromises the integrity and scope of its witness. Indeed, the consequences of denying creative therapeutic space to God's children are personal and corporate, temporal and eternal.

In person-centered pastoral care, caregivers nurture creative space for healing and growth, all for the sake of empowering people with intellectual disabilities to embrace the unique vocations to which God has called them. While person-centered pastoral caregivers need to be mindful of the vocational framework that shapes their ministry, they must also be mindful that theirs is a fundamentally interdisciplinary ministry. As such, while theological realities will inevitably be at the forefront of their minds, person-centered pastoral caregivers must also understand how person-centered thinking functions psychologically in their practices of care. Specifically, there are three main components of object-relations theory that fund the psychological architecture of person-centered pastoral care: the holding environment (a safe, supportive space), the cultivation of true and false selves, and the necessity of mutual creativity through play.

MAKING ROOM: THE HOLDING ENVIRONMENT AND "GOOD-ENOUGH" CARE

A caring relationship based on person-centered thinking functions as a safe, collaborative space within which people with intellectual disabilities can turn their dreams into realities. Unlike managed space, which is controlled by an outside authority and its system of rules and regulations, or private space, which is characterized by individualism and isolation, shared space is sustained by a belief in interdependence and a commitment to teamwork and collaboration. Furthermore, shared space is nurtured and protected by supportive caregivers who are committed to helping people with intellectual disabilities find ways to live full and authentic lives. The inhabitants of shared space focus on identifying an individual's giftedness—his or her contribution to society—and the ways in which others can help the individual to share his or her gifts with the larger community.[1] In shared space an individual's particular needs and dreams are of primary concern—not the needs or agendas of family members, therapists, or other support personnel. In this way, the care receiver has ownership of the therapeutic process.

Through collaboration with caregivers in a safe, shared space, care receivers can explore their gifts and interests and imagine ways of sharing these gifts with their community.

In psychological terms, person-centered care is "good-enough" care. A mother's good-enough care for her child equips the child to emerge from infancy as an individual who can conceive of himself or herself as separate from his or her mother and who can live authentically in the world. Conversely, the absence of good-enough mothering can compromise a child's—and an adult's—ability to live an authentic, fulfilling life of his or her own. Similarly, in relationships between caregivers and care receivers, the caregivers strive to provide good-enough care such that the care receivers emerge from the caring relationship with a greater degree of self-understanding and, hopefully, a greater capacity to live lives commensurate with who they really are.

Good-enough care requires good-enough space. In the relationship between an infant and a "good-enough mother," the mother's care is a safe "space" in which the mother tends to her infant's every need with careful attention and empathy.[2] In this "holding environment" that the mother creates for her infant, the mother does not impose on the infant her own assumptions about the infant's needs. She works with her infant to ensure that the infant's actual needs are met. The interaction between mother and infant is fundamentally and necessarily creative; in addition to supplying all of her infant's needs, a good-enough mother nurtures the infant's developing self.[3] In a carefully choreographed dance between supply and demand, the mother provides for her infant in a way that allows the infant the illusion of supplying his or her own needs. By nurturing this sense of self-sufficiency, the good-enough mother prepares her infant to conceive of himself or herself as an independent being who can interact with the world.[4]

Just as a mother's attentive, creative care nurtures her infant's sense of self, a good-enough, person-centered caregiver's care evokes positive change, growth, and healing when the care receiver's particular needs shape the therapeutic intervention. Whether a care receiver's needs are traumatic or relatively benign, they are best addressed on the care receiver's terms.[5] Rather than trying to force the caregiver's own interpretation of the care receiver's particular issue, the good-enough caregiver pays close attention to the needs, feelings, and issues of the care receiver and offers interpretation and other forms of care in a manner in keeping with the clues that the care receiver has given. A good-enough mother knows the needs of her child and adapts her modes of care to those needs. Similarly, in their more sophisticated interactions, a good-enough caregiver takes the time to learn the needs of the care receiver, adapt to those needs, and nurture the kind of creative space wherein the caregiver and care receiver can together find clarity and move the care receiver toward healing. A good-enough pastoral caregiver does not simply offer words of wisdom and expect the care receiver to blithely absorb the words and move along. The caregiver does not presume to have all the answers. Instead, a good-enough caregiver willingly joins in a delicate dance with a care receiver, paying close attention to the care receiver's cues and only offering interpretation and feedback at appropriate moments in the conversation. The caregiver may not have enough information to offer the care receiver any helpful interpretations of the care receiver's material. Interestingly, though, the caregiver's powerlessness is actually important to and helpful for the care receiver. The caregiver's inability to control the conversation preserves for the care receiver a sense of control that is crucial to the care receiver's growth as a person and reinforces the truly collaborative nature of their caring relationship.

In the relationship between a good-enough mother and her infant, the mother is a facilitator who creatively nurtures the emergence of her infant's true self. However, in a good-enough, person-centered caring relationship, the caregiver and care receiver are equal partners in the therapeutic process. Certainly, the care receiver uses his or her expertise to facilitate the process. Good-enough caregivers pay close attention to their care receivers' needs at any given moment and adjust their own modes of communication accordingly. Even so, the purpose of these adjustments is to preserve the authentic therapeutic collaboration between the caregivers and care receivers. For example, if a care receiver seems anxious or frustrated when a caregiver asks a series of questions about a particular issue or concern, a good-enough caregiver might employ a mode of communication with which the care receiver can more comfortably engage. The caregiver might invite the care receiver to suggest an activity that the two of them can do together. A care receiver who is interested in art might suggest that the caregiver join him in coloring pictures, while a musician might invite her caregiver to join in listening to songs by her favorite band. By allowing the care receiver to shape the collaboration and set the pace of the communication, the person-centered caregiver instills a sense of respect and trust in the caring relationship and paves the way for future collaboration.

A good-enough, person-centered caregiver relinquishes control of the therapeutic relationship in exchange for collaboration and partnership with the care receiver. Occasions may arise in which good-enough care demands that a caregiver reclaim control of the therapeutic relationship for the sake of the care receiver's specific needs in that moment. Nevertheless, the good-enough caregiver maintains a commitment to being a partner in the care receiver's journey toward healing.[6] After all, the space they share ultimately belongs to the care receiver and his or her unique hopes and dreams. To this ownership—and owner—the good-enough caregiver remains true.

NURTURING THE TRUE SELF

Creative care offered in a safe space and shaped by the particularities of the care receiver enables a care receiver's true self to find expression. In the relationship between a "good-enough" mother and her infant, the mother affords her infant the opportunities for creativity that are so vital to his or her development. A good-enough mother allows her infant to believe that the infant has created an object that will meet his or her need (a nourishing breast or, later, a soft, comforting piece of cloth or stuffed animal). The mother's empathic care and her willingness to allow the infant's illusion nourish the infant's true self.[7] When the mother allows her infant the freedom to operate according to his or her own unique dreams, the infant becomes equipped to live authentically and meaningfully in the world.

A good-enough mother uses illusion as a creative tool with which to equip her infant to embrace his or her own strengths and live a meaningful life. For care receivers in a therapeutic setting, good-enough care is as creative as a mother's care, yet it does not simply supply care receivers with the illusion that they can cultivate meaningful lives for themselves. Instead, good-enough caregivers engage care receivers in creative encounters that enable the care receivers not only to discover their own strengths and possibilities but also to participate in finding ways to activate them. While good-enough care is creative to its core, care that is "not good-enough" is fundamentally uncreative.[8] People with intellectual disabilities are often the recipients of uncreative care that meets their basic physical needs but fails to attend creatively to the unique dreams and wishes they have for their lives. Consequently, many people with intellectual disabilities move through life under the influence of compliant false selves that obscure their true selves and lead them to simply do as they are told and accept the care that they are given.[9] When care receivers' true selves are hidden, the care receivers may not receive the kind of care and support that they really need because their compliant false selves are all that anyone sees.[10]

Compliance is as much a learned behavior in people with intellectual disabilities as it is in infants. For example, an infant learns compliance—and develops a false self—when the infant's mother fails to provide good-enough care. By insisting on meeting the infant's needs on her own terms, the mother lures her infant into accepting her care whether or not the care is what the infant actually needs at that moment.[11] The mother's actions cultivate the infant's false self and, consequently, disable the infant's capacity for authenticity. Guided by a false, inauthentic self, the infant cultivates false, inauthentic relationships with others. Like a chameleon, the infant takes on the characteristics and preferences of the dominant people in his or her life at any given moment instead of displaying the unique qualities of his or her true self.[12] The infant's adaptation to others— especially to his or her mother—is a self-protective attempt to preserve relationships with caregivers and avoid the abandonment the infant so greatly fears. Successful self-protection, however, comes at great cost to the infant, as the spontaneity and creativity so characteristic of the true self are buried beneath compliance and imitation.[13]

Like infants, people with intellectual disabilities often have little to no power in caring relationships; their caregivers simply address perceived deficiencies instead of cultivating strengths.[14] Care marked by power imbalances and forced compliance can lead people with intellectual disabilities to engage in behaviors shaped by their false selves. Stories abound of people with disabilities who will do anything to get what they want or who play one support staff person against another. A closer look at so-called "manipulative" people with disabilities and their behaviors may reveal people who are determined to get what they want but who must resort to less-than-ideal tactics to achieve the desired outcome. In other words, inappropriate behavior in a person with intellectual disability may reflect the hidden presence of a true self that is desperate to find expression.

Inappropriate behavior can reflect the triumph of a false self in people with intellectual disabilities, but so can silence and inaction. Like infants and children desperate to preserve their relationships with their primary caregivers, people with intellectual disabilities often simply avoid expressing their true thoughts and feelings about certain issues because they are afraid of being abandoned by people who care for them. They may agree to participate in certain activities or conversations with people simply because they do not want to be alone. For example, a person with little to no religious involvement or commitment might accept a chaplain's invitation to talk simply because he or she is lonely and may even feign an interest in spiritual matters. Caregivers working with care receivers who exhibit either negative or passive behavior must communicate, through both word and deed, that the care receiver's true self is valuable and worth exploring together in a caring partnership marked by mutual respect and shared responsibility. Part of the effectiveness of good-enough, person-centered care lies in the balance of power between a caregiver and a care receiver. A person-centered caregiver shares power with the care receiver.[15] When power is shared equally between a caregiver and a care receiver, the care receiver becomes a participant in his or her own process of healing and growth. A caring relationship marked by a balance of power is one in which a person's true self is respected and nurtured.

MUTUAL CREATIVITY THROUGH PLAY: THE LIFEBLOOD OF GOOD-ENOUGH CARE

The shape of the caring relationship plays a fundamental role in a care receiver's ability to discover and embrace his or her true self. A caring relationship in which the care receiver wields all power is the kind of relationship that thwarts authenticity and safeguards the triumph of a care receiver's false self. On the other hand, care shaped by creativity, collaboration, and play can inspire a care receiver to share his or her true self with the caregiver and, hopefully, with the world.

Even infants need creative, playful care from a caregiver who is willing to share in the playing. The space between a good-enough mother and her infant is, in essence, a playroom, because it is here, in this space, that an infant begins to play.[16] An infant's playroom is a peculiar space. It is not solely a product of the infant's inner world, nor is it merely a fixture in the infant's external reality. Instead, an infant's playroom is an intermediate space in which both internal and external realities fund the play that happens there.[17] The playroom is a place of relaxation in which the infant plays freely as a means of making sense of himself or herself as well as the world.[18] The infant's play is not subjected to any external rules; rather, the infant is free to create and to simply be.

The collaborative play between mother and infant is crucial to the infant's development. The infant plays with objects that symbolize the infant's union with his or her mother, and the mother plays along, allowing the infant to believe that he or she has created these objects and controls them.[19] The mother's loving, reliable presence strengthens the infant's ego, as does her participation in her infant's play. This same capacity to use symbols that is nurtured in an infant's play with transitional objects finds its way into practices of caring with both children and adults. While a child's symbolic, therapeutic play often involves blocks, dolls, or other toys, an adult care receiver may "play" with art, words, or ideas as resources with which to work through feelings, life struggles, and dreams. Using images from poetry, paintings, or other works of art, adults can relax and play, giving expression to who they are and who they would like to be.[20]

Essential to a care receiver's successful self-discovery through play is a caregiver's equally playful collaboration. A person-centered caregiver assumes the role of playmate and desires for the care receiver to share responsibility for the work (or, rather, play) that transpires between them. To be sure, the playful caregiver does not abandon attempts to interpret the care receiver's words and actions. Instead, the caregiver allows interpretations of the care receiver's material to emerge from their mutual play, making sure that the interpretations accurately reflect the care receiver's thoughts and actions.[21] Playful, collaborative caregiving nourishes the sense of trust that has been or is being established between caregiver and care receiver and, in so doing, enables a care receiver to feel comfortable sharing his or her true self.[22] The caregiver's trustworthiness, coupled with his or her willingness to engage the care receiver as a partner in the work of play, communicates respect for the care receiver and empowers the care receiver to explore life's true potential.[23]

Person-centered care invites and empowers a care receiver to be creative—to play, to dream, to explore the possibilities that life can offer. The creativity that is at the heart of play is vital to all human flourishing. The act of "being creative" may involve the creation of a work of art or the composition of a piece of music, but it may also include much more. "Being creative" means living creatively.[24] Creative living brings with it a sense of aliveness in body, mind, and spirit, as well as a personal ethos of authenticity, and it signals the triumph of the true self. Uncreative living, by contrast, is a way of life in which a person's false self is in charge. A person living uncreatively lives a life of adaptation and compliance driven by the expectations of others instead of the desires of his or her own heart.[25] A person who lives uncreatively is a person who has not been allowed to play. An uncreative life is a life void of the opportunities for self-expression and discovery that play affords.

Creativity signals that an individual is truly alive—and truly living.[26] If, in fact, creativity is an essential criterion for an authentically lived life but is only measured by a person's capacity for particular limited forms of self-expression, then many people with intellectual disabilities—particularly people with profound intellectual disabilities—might be considered incapable of truly living.[27] Creativity, however, is not simply a human attribute that some people possess and others lack. Creativity is an activity, an engagement between a human being and his or her environment.[28] An individual's ability or inability to live creatively has at least as much to do with his or her surroundings as it does with cognitive function. When people with intellectual disabilities have difficulty participating in community life, the difficulty often comes from a lack of community support—the kind of support that is essential to creative living. A person's capacity for self-discovery and self-expression through creativity is largely dependent on other people and the ways in which they either promote or sabotage the process. People who do not believe that people with intellectual disabilities can take part in community life sabotage the process of self-discovery for people with intellectual disabilities. Intellectual disability and creativity—including creative care—are only mutually exclusive if the environment itself is uncreative—that is, if the community is unable to imagine ways in which its members with disabilities might discover their gifts and use them to make positive contributions to the community. Disability does not hinder creativity, but uncreative communities can.[29]

Just as an infant or young child is dependent on others to nurture his or her healthy development, all people, including people with disabilities, need a supportive community that can nurture self-discovery by encouraging and enabling creative living. Self-discovery is a community endeavor. In the safe, unchallenged space nurtured by his or her community of support, a person with disabilities and his or her community "play" together. Through their creative interaction, persons and their communities together discover each person's true self and his or her hopes for an authentic and meaningful life.

PERSON-CENTERED CARE: A GOOD-ENOUGH, CREATIVE COLLABORATION

Person-centered care involves the kind of playful, collaborative care that object-relations psychology champions. In all person-centered care, one or more good-enough caregivers nurture a safe, unchallenged space that is shaped solely by the particular needs of the care receiver. In this space, caregivers join with care receivers in mutual play, during which they partner together in exploring the care receivers' dreams, nightmares, gifts, and the images they evoke. No dream is too outlandish or impossible to be shared and explored. The play of person-centered care is hospitable play that invites and even necessitates the full participation of both caregivers and care receivers. Caregivers play with care receivers in such a way that the care receivers can take ownership of this creative process and its outcomes. Just as the holding environment is a "resting place" for a developing infant to play freely, a caring, person-centered space welcomes the kind of easy, playful activity that facilitates a care receiver's authentic self-expression. In a person-centered pastoral care relationship, the care receiver does not have to feel as if he or she is being interviewed or interrogated, as the sense of "being on" in a therapeutic encounter can breed anxiety and prevent the care receiver from sharing his or her true self with the caregiver. Instead, care receivers in person-centered relationships are invited to meander through their thoughts via free association, communicating ideas, impulses, and sensations that may or may not be connected in any noticeable way.[30] The stream-of-consciousness communication that is encouraged in person-centered care allows the care receiver to share himself or herself creatively without the threat of judgment, and it allows the care receiver to move ever closer to discovering his or her true self.[31] In the safe space that person-centered caregivers create, care receivers are free to imagine, dream, and express their authentic selves. In so doing, care receivers can discover who they are, as well as who they want to be.

Like a child's activities in a playroom, the shape of person-centered support can take different forms. In the field of disability services, person-centered support often takes the form of a playgroup, in which a care receiver and his or her most trusted family members, friends, and support professionals (a "circle of support") play together to uncover the care receiver's needs and dreams for his or her life and to name the nightmares that the care receiver wants to avoid. The "toys" that shape the group's activities are questions designed to guide the process of play. The questions explore the care receiver's personal history, interests, gifts and talents, needs, dreams, and nightmares. After exploring the answers to these questions, the group begins to create a concrete plan by which the care receiver can avoid his or her nightmares from happening and enable the dreams to become reality. While there may be a group facilitator to help the group stay on task, the care receiver and his or her playmates control the conversation.[32]

Person-centered support can occur in a playgroup, but it can also take place during a playdate—a simple partnership between one caregiver and one care receiver. Direct support providers for people with disabilities frequently utilize person-centered resources in their relationships with the people they support. Direct support providers assist people with disabilities with many, if not all, of their essential daily tasks and needs, including bathing, dressing, eating, toileting, transportation, communication, fixing meals, and housekeeping. These one-on-one relationships are essential. The shape of these relationships can have a profound impact on how people with disabilities see themselves and envision their lives—both present and future.[33] Direct support providers who incorporate person-centered ideas in their work do not simply carry out the duties for which they are compensated. Rather, they value getting to know the care receiver through shared daily experiences. When a direct support provider chooses to engage in conversation with a care receiver in order to learn more about him or her, the direct support provider can discover the care receiver's values, as well as the dreams and goals the care receiver has for his or her life.[34] The direct support relationship is transformed into a partnership grounded in genuine respect. Care borne out of a meaningful direct support relationship demonstrates that the care receiver is truly seen and heard. The care receiver's true self is empowered to speak instead of being silenced by the assumptions and projections of a disengaged caregiver.[35] A direct support relationship guided by person-centered thinking is quite different from the support relationships that many people with disabilities experience because it is characterized by a spirit of mutuality. In a person-centered direct support relationship, the caregiver and care receiver play together to ensure that the care receiver has the best possible support. Through their collaborative play, the care receiver is empowered to be their best and most authentic self.[36]

When direct support providers partner with care receivers in practices of care, the care receivers may feel respected and heard in ways they never have before. In some cases, direct support providers extend their play to include assisting care receivers in discovering their gifts and articulating their dreams. A direct support provider for a care receiver who does not speak may use photographs, magazine clippings, and symbolic objects to enable the care receiver to communicate his or her interests and hopes. The direct support provider nurtures a safe, unchallenged environment in which to engage in collaborative play with the care receiver. A person-centered direct support provider's creativity, respect, and collaboration enable the care receiver's true self to emerge and find expression.[37] Even though specific forms of person-centered support have been developed to guide the support process for people with disabilities, person-centered care is more than a simple therapeutic technique. Person-centered care is, above all, an art form. Using the medium of deep listening, a person-centered caregiver can piece together the images and symbols that a care receiver shares and uncover the care receiver's hopes, dreams, concerns, and fears. A person-centered caregiver's careful, hospitable listening fosters transformation, not simply in the life of the care receiver but also in the relationship between the care receiver and his or her community.[38] As a care receiver's hopes and dreams are heard, they can be woven into the fabric of the care receiver's life through new routines and activities. The transformed life—the work of art—that emerges from a person-centered caring relationship is a life that more accurately reflects the care receiver's authentic self, rather than a false self or, worse, a person or agency who might otherwise control the care receiver's life and future. When images become action through collaborative, person-centered support, people with intellectual disabilities have the opportunity to realize their dreams for their lives.[39]

ROOM FOR THE HOLY: FINDING GOD IN GOOD-ENOUGH CARE

In good-enough, person-centered pastoral care, a caregiver and care receiver play together in a safe, unchallenged space, exploring as partners the images and ideas that reflect the care receiver's dreams and nightmares. The imaginative space of person-centered pastoral care is also a place in which a caregiver and care receiver can "play" in matters of faith and engage with the holy.[40] A person-centered relationship between a pastoral caregiver and care receiver is similar to person-centered relationships between other types of support providers (therapists and direct support workers) and the people they support. However, in the caring relationships between a *pastoral* caregiver and care receiver, issues of faith—as well as images of God—may find expression more readily than they do in other caring relationships. Issues of faith and images of God inevitably inform the dreams and nightmares that care receivers convey and thus shape the play that transpires between the pastoral caregiver and the care receiver. Matters of faith and God can function both theologically and psychologically in therapeutic relationships and in person-centered pastoral care. As caregivers and care receivers join together in playing with matters of faith, they may discover that thoughts and ideas about God and faith are manifesting in unexpected ways. The care receiver may reveal personal images of God that reflect the presence of an issue or conflict in the care receiver's life that needs to be explored psychologically. On the other hand, pastoral play between caregiver and care receiver might reveal a care receiver's struggle with forgiveness or shame, in which case biblical and theological resources might best facilitate a more focused exploration of the care receiver's concerns.

The relationship between a person-centered pastoral caregiver and a care receiver functions as a safe, creative playroom in which there is plenty of room and grace to explore both what is worldly and what is holy. The access to an unchallenged transitional space that is so essential in an infant's development remains essential throughout a person's life and is an essential component of good-enough pastoral care. Like an infant's playroom, this space is a "third area of experiencing" that is neither internal nor external reality yet includes both. This psychic playroom is the space to which people of all ages retreat as they engage their imaginations in artistic experiences—and in religious activity.[41] Participation in religious practices—including pastoral care—is a kind of play. In the practice of pastoral care, caregivers and care receivers consider or "play with" images of and ideas about God that emerge from both human experience and religious tradition. In a person-centered pastoral care relationship, a caregiver and care receiver join together in reverent play with the divine. Through their intentional, reverent play with images of and ideas about God, care receivers can explore and deepen their understandings of God, themselves, and the world, and caregivers can help facilitate care receivers' friendship with the God who both fills and transcends human experience.

The subjective images of God that may be considered in person-centered play derive from everyday life experiences, including dreams, encounters with nature, and relationships with others.[42] A person's subjective God-images are important and necessary because they reflect the person's ego back to himself or herself. However, the self-reflection that a subjective God-image provides can be a blessing or curse; while it may sometimes effect positive, peaceful moments of self-awareness, it can also be a source of judgment, admonishing its custodian and exposing his or her inadequacies. For example, a young woman whose father abandoned her as a child might hold on to an image of a God who is distant at best, or at worst, absent. She may feel that her disability is proof that God does not love her and is not with her. Conversely, a young man who experienced a traumatic and unstable childhood might cling to the image of a God who is close to him and who speaks to him constantly, guiding his actions through both words and visions. He may understand his disability as part of God's plan for his life—and thus as one of the only challenges in his life that makes sense. In both positive and negative ways, subjective God-images play important roles in people's lives and undergird their beliefs in God, however strong or tenuous the beliefs might be.[43] Subjective God-images are as unique as the people to whom they belong. Some people hold subjective God-images that bring them comfort and hope. For others, their personal image of God evokes feelings of judgment, hopelessness, and despair.[44]

While subjective images of God emerge from personal experience, objective images of God derive from the doctrines, histories, and scriptures that constitute religious traditions.[45] Objective God-images are more comprehensive than subjective God-images because they derive from countless people's and communities' interpretations of scripture, their theological controversies, and their imaginations.[46] Precisely because they emerge from a patchwork of communities and interpretations throughout history, objective images of God are complex at best. The complexity of objective God-images inevitably informs person-centered pastoral care with people with disabilities because Judeo-Christian scripture offers a complex witness on the subject. On the one hand, scripture depicts a God who calls Moses, a man who is "slow of speech and slow of tongue" (Exodus 4:10), to lead God's people out of Egypt. On the other hand, scripture presents the image of a God whose Law ostensibly prohibits a number of people and groups—including people with deformities—from becoming priests (Leviticus 21:16-23). Care receivers who are seeking to find meaning for their lives as people with disabilities may want to "play" with these and other disability-related texts in the safe space of a person-centered pastoral care relationship. Likewise, caregivers might draw from church history, hagiography, or various theological movements to help illuminate aspects of life, faith, and disability for care receivers.

A vibrant life of faith necessitates attention to both objective and subjective God-images. Attention to only the objective God-images derived from tradition produces a compliant faith that looks good but lacks the joy that comes through a personal encounter with a living God. On the other hand, attending only to personal experiences of God and ignoring the God of tradition can compromise a person's capacity to have faith in something beyond himself or herself.[47] A playful, person-centered approach to pastoral care is an approach that takes all God-images seriously—those that derive from personal experiences as well as those received from tradition. A care receiver's dreams and nightmares will likely find expression, in some way, in his or her personal images of God.[48] Similarly, an exploration of objective God-images drawn from centuries-old testimonies and traditions can foster a sense of self-understanding and hope that may help a care receiver see his or her life—and self—as worthwhile. For example, a young man with a physical deformity in his feet believes he is a disappointment to his father, who desperately wants him to be an athlete. The father's displeasure fosters in the young man an inferiority complex and a sense of failure. One day, while touring a church in a foreign country, the young man sees a mosaic depicting Christ ruling over the earth. To the young man, Christ's toes look like talons and thus resemble his own toes. The sight of the resurrected Christ ruling over all with feet just like those of the young man enabled the young man to look at his own feet—and at himself—with love and appreciation instead of failure and inadequacy.[49]

Important discoveries can take place in a pastoral care relationship as a caregiver and care receiver play with and explore subjective and objective images of God. Over time, as a person's psyche moves back and forth in its consideration of opposite and potentially conflicting attitudes, images, or instincts, a third psychic component emerges. The new component includes the two original competing options yet is at the same time distinct and transcends the original conflict.[50] The new component is a bigger center—a new, true self that corresponds to the deepest core of the personality. This self is not something that the person has created. Rather, the new, true self corresponds to the deepest core of the personality. It is the true and authentic self that transcends anything created out of a person's dreams or nightmares.[51] The true and authentic self is the self that God created, the self to whom God has given a particular vocation. This is the self for whose life God has dreams of God's own.

By playing with the various images of God that a care receiver brings to the pastoral care playroom, the caregiver and care receiver may be able to meet the care receiver's true, God-given self. In the midst of their holy play, the caregiver and care receiver may meet God as well. Just as a person's true self is made known in the midst of the psyche's playful movement between ideas and images, God may make God's self known in the pastoral playroom, as caregivers and care receivers move playfully between subjective and objective images of God. God meets God's playful people as the God who, while ultimately transcendent, reveals God's self in every intimate detail of a person's life—in and through dreams, illness, health, and all areas of human subjectivity and particularity.[52] In the space between subjective and objective images of God, the true God—who is at once immanent and transcendent—may not only meet God's children but may also join them in their play.

All people—including people with intellectual disabilities—need access to these creative spaces where they may exercise their freedom to dream. Person-centered care is care that honors dreams and believes in the dreamers. Person-centered caregivers understand themselves to be collaborative partners in the sacred task of unearthing a care receiver's authentic self and finding concrete ways for the care receiver to share this self with the world. Person-centered pastoral caregivers are particularly attuned to the sacredness of their collaboration with their care receivers and recognize that the selves they are trying to unearth do not belong to agencies, institutions, or other caregivers. The selves that person-centered pastoral caregivers are trying to unearth in their care receivers are the selves that God created, called good, and endowed with unique—and uniquely important—vocations. In a pastoral care relationship, a pastoral caregiver and care receiver play together with the care receiver's needs, dreams, nightmares, and understandings of

God. In the sacred space of a person-centered pastoral care relationship, the care receiver's true, God-given self is free to find expression. In the sacred space of person-centered pastoral care, God can reveal God's self and God's great dreams for God's people.

SUGGESTIONS FOR FURTHER READING

Falvey, Mary, Marsha Forest, Jack Pearpoint, and Richard Rosenberg. *All My Life's a Circle: Using the Tools—Circles, MAPS and PATHS.* Toronto: Inclusion Press, 1997.

O'Brien, John, and Connie Lyle O'Brien, eds. *Implementing Person-Centered Planning: Voices of Experience.* Toronto: Inclusion Press, 2002.

Ulanov, Ann Belford. *Finding Space: God, Winnicott, and Psychic Reality.* Louisville, Ky.: Westminster John Knox, 2001.

Winnicott, D. W. *Playing and Reality.* London: Routledge, 2006.

3

Calling
The Theology of Person-Centered Pastoral Care

Judeo-Christian scripture is replete with reminders that all things are possible with God. In the book of Exodus, a body of water parts so that God's enslaved people can escape to freedom. In the Gospel of John, Jesus multiplies the meager contents of a young boy's lunch box and feeds thousands of hungry people. And, perhaps most audaciously, Luke's Gospel tells the story of a young Jewish virgin who conceives and bears a child whose life, death, and "impossible" resurrection forever change the shape and telos of every human life. Scripture affirms that anything is possible with God and that *anyone* can be an agent of God's kingdom work. Everyone has a unique, important, God-given vocation, including people with the most profound intellectual disabilities. Christopher de Vinck bears witness to the compatibility of vocation and disability in his account of the life of his brother Oliver who was born with multiple developmental and intellectual disabilities. Because of the profundity of Oliver's disabilities, physicians advised de Vinck's parents to institutionalize Oliver for the duration of what would likely be a very short life. Rather than taking the physicians' advice, the de Vincks opted to take their son home to rear him and love him—just as they had done with all their other children.[1]

Oliver de Vinck's physical and intellectual disabilities did not prevent him from making unique and vital contributions to his family, to his community, and to society at large. Christopher de Vinck received many written responses to his published accounts of life with Oliver (which first appeared as magazine and newspaper articles), including letters from the president, other national dignitaries, and religious leaders. Oliver's seemingly powerless and hopeless life bore witness to the fact that profound intellectual disability does not prevent someone from holding an important place in a family, in a community, and even in a church.[2] Despite his many physical and intellectual limitations, Oliver had a calling that was just as meaningful as those of his more able-bodied and able-minded brothers, sisters, and parents. Oliver was called to a life of fellowship with God, lived out through discipleship and witness. Oliver was faithful to that call, even though he had a profound intellectual disability. Oliver's faithfulness was enacted in, through, and because of his relationships with others. Oliver was not presumed to be—to cite the contentious term used by one of De Vinck's students to describe Oliver—simply a "vegetable."[3] He was recognized as someone who had gifts to offer his family, his community, and his God (he was baptized and confirmed in the Catholic Church). He was given the space to be a brother, a son, a friend, and even an advocate. Oliver had a calling, and within that calling he had a particular vocation. With the help of those who knew him best and loved him most, Oliver lived out both.

Thanks to Oliver de Vinck's stalwart circle of support, he was able to live out his God-given life to its fullest and most faithful extent. The same kind of creativity and collaboration that shaped Oliver's care is at the heart of person-centered pastoral care. In person-centered pastoral care, a caregiver and a care receiver collaborate—or play together—in what is best described as a pastoral friendship. The pastoral friendship can be the locus of an encounter with the God who has created and called all of God's children to be God's friends and witnesses. In a pastoral friendship, a caregiver and care receiver can partner together to discover God's carefully crafted dreams for each of their lives.

Person-centered pastoral friendships are not simply safe spaces; they are sacred spaces. They are sacred spaces because they are grounded in sacred friendship—in God's friendship. God calls all of God's children to become Christians and live faithfully in friendship with God.[4] A person-centered pastoral friendship mediates the friendship with God to which all people are called. It is a sacred space where

God can make God's presence and love known and where, through the power of the Holy Spirit, vocation can come to life.

CALLED, CHOSEN, EMPOWERED

In pastoral friendships, intellectual disability is not a barrier to friendship or faith. Nevertheless, questions still arise regarding the extent to which people with intellectual disabilities can be obedient to God's call and live out their particular vocations. Given the nature of God's actions toward human beings, questions regarding agency and people with disabilities reflect a general misunderstanding about the agent who is at work in the process of calling. Calling and vocation are gifts from God, not products of human agency. While Christian scripture offers mixed messages regarding people with disabilities and their identity in the kingdom of God, the scriptures are quite clear that God's calling has no respect for persons and does not depend on human action.[5] God calls all of God's children, regardless of ability or disability. In John 15:16 Jesus says to his disciples, "You did not choose me but I chose you. And I appointed you to go and bear fruit, fruit that will last." The foundation of God's calling to human beings is their election in Jesus Christ, not anything they have done or can do on their own. Before any human act of reaching to God, God reaches out to God's children and calls each one to be in fellowship with God.[6] Through human beings' election in Christ, God makes known God's ardent intention that all of God's children be in fellowship with God. In and through Christ, all human beings have been claimed as covenant partners with God.[7] God's calling on every human life, then, is purely a gift of grace from a God who seeks out God's children to be God's friends.[8]

Just as no one has done or can do anything to deserve or effect his or her election, salvation, and reconciliation, no one can do anything on his or her own to be faithful to God's call to friendship with God. God has always been a friend to God's people, and God's friendship with God's people is a gift that is offered independent of and prior to anyone's response to it.[9] Even so, God does enable all people to answer God's calling and receive the gift of God's friendship. Calling is not contingent upon a person's intellectual capabilities, and neither is the ability to be obedient. Calling is an act of God in Christ, and human beings' ability to be faithful to it is an act of the Holy Spirit.[10] It is not people's work but God's work through the Holy Spirit that makes all people—including people with disabilities—capable of answering God's call.

The Mechanics of God's Call

Because God is the sole agent who calls, the event of calling eludes human description or classification and defies human logic.[11] Calling is a mystery. In all of God's mysterious creativity, God alone calls God's people, employing whatever means necessary to guarantee that God will be heard and answered. Two metaphors derived from human experience facilitate human attempts to describe the indescribable event of calling. Calling may be a kind of "illumination," in which God's light shines on a person and enables him or her to claim God's love and grace.[12] Calling could also be a sort of "awakening," in which a person's spiritual eyes are opened in a way that allows him or her to recognize and embrace true life marked by God's work in Christ.[13] God may use various aspects of the human experience to facilitate the event of calling. God may choose to illuminate God's people through the ancient testimonies of prophets and apostles. God may awaken God's people through an act of preaching or a celebration of the sacraments.[14] However, if God stops at nothing to guarantee that all of God's people hear God's call, then God will not simply appeal to human reason and will when calling God's children to friendship. In this post-Enlightenment world, the faculty of human reason is often lauded to a fault and believed to be essential to human flourishing. To insist that reason and will are essential to human flourishing and Christian faithfulness, though, is to deny the value of people who lack the capacity for reason and will but who are, nevertheless, children of God for whom Christ died and with whom God desires friendship.

God's calling makes possible the things that are, by human estimations, impossible; God's logic baffles human logic and turns it on its head.[15] Through the power of the Holy Spirit, God calls and enables people with even the most profound intellectual disabilities to be friends with God.[16] In all of God's creative mystery, God speaks to, "illuminates," or "awakens" the whole person: the body, the senses, and the mind—not simply the intellect.[17] God may choose to illuminate a person with an intellectual disability by appealing to his or her sense of hearing using an encounter with a hymn or another kind of musical composition to convey God's love and grace. God could awaken someone else through his or her sense of sight by using an encounter with an icon, sculpture, or other work of art to bring him or her closer to God. Or, perhaps, within the sacred space of a pastoral friendship, God could use the intentional mutual play between human friends to awaken one or both of them so that they can embrace the joy of friendship with God.

The Telos of Calling

When God calls a person, God intends for the person to become a Christian, and being a Christian means being in fellowship with the God who calls.[18] The fact that friendship with God is the *telos* of God's calling reflects the nature of God who, as Father, Son, and Holy Spirit, is fundamentally relational.[19] The shape of the friendship to which God calls God's children is discipleship. All of God's children are called to a life of friendship with God as disciples of Jesus Christ. People who are friends with God belong to Jesus; he, as their Lord, has claimed them.[20] Christians are united to Christ as his friends and are drawn into a relationship marked by close and genuine fellowship.[21] Since all people have been determined for this friendship, all people are capable of entering into it and, thus, into God's prophetic work. In and through Christ, God calls all people and enables their obedience.

OBEDIENCE AND ANTHROPOLOGY

While God alone is at work in the event of calling, the person who is called needs to offer a response to God's call.[22] A person's response to God's call is, to be sure, a tremendous leap of faith—a leap that may, on the surface, seem unfair and, in some cases, impossible for people with intellectual disabilities. However, just as it is God alone who is at work in the event of calling, it is God alone who equips and empowers God's children to move forward in faith and obedience.[23] The same creative God who can illuminate and awaken every human heart—including those that belong to people with intellectual disabilities—can fill those hearts with courage, enabling them to say yes to God's call and follow wherever God leads.[24] Thus, a person's ability to be faithful to God's call comes not from himself or herself but rather from the God who seeks out God's people for friendship.

Leaping and Intellectual Disability

A person's leap of obedience to God's call should not be taken in fear but in confidence. The Christian can answer God's call in the affirmative, knowing that the God who asks for faith is the same God who, by the power of the Holy Spirit, enables the Christian to be faithful. At the same time, however, each Christian must assume a measure of responsibility in the task of faithfulness. Faithfulness, by its very definition, necessitates a personal response from the faithful. Therefore, every Christian must take the leap in answering God's calling—and must do it on his or her own.[25] Viewed through the lens of intellectual disability, the notion of a personal response of obedience to God's call seems not only daunting but also unhelpful and even irrelevant. Some individuals living with intellectual disability do have the capacity for reason and will and can make conscious, overt faith decisions. People living with more profound intellectual disabilities lack these faculties. If Christians insist that a certain capacity for reason and will is essential for obedience to vocation, then they deny the fact that a person with a profound intellectual disability can and should participate in the Christian life, not to mention the work of the church.[26]

The notion of obedience to call is challenging for people with intellectual disabilities precisely because of common perspectives held by Christians without intellectual disabilities. Some Christians question the need for people with intellectual disabilities to make any sort of faith decision at all, while others argue that a faith decision is simply impossible. When Christians believe that people with intellectual disabilities do not need to make a faith decision, they effectively place people with intellectual disabilities on a spiritual pedestal and implicitly exempt them from the responsibilities that come with Christian discipleship.[27] To be sure, the notion that people with intellectual disabilities are "holy innocents" is certainly preferable to earlier perspectives that attributed the cause of disability to sin or demonic possession. Nevertheless, conceiving of people with intellectual disabilities as holy innocents effectively situates them above humanity, thereby allowing people to accept them without acknowledging that they, too, are fully human.[28]

While some Christians view people with intellectual disabilities as being above humanity and therefore exempt from human responsibility before God, others imply that people with intellectual disabilities are less than human and question their ability to be active participants in a life of faith. Far too frequently people with intellectual disabilities have been barred from taking communion or participating in other faith practices because they could not demonstrate that they actually understood what they were doing.[29] The assertion that people with intellectual disabilities have neither the need nor the ability to take the leap of faith in answering God's call not only robs them of the opportunity to claim what God has for them but also denies their identity as children of God who have been created for and called to friendship with God and neighbor. Contrary to all-too-common beliefs, even people with the most profound intellectual disabilities can—and do—respond faithfully to the God who calls them.

I Jump, You Jump: Leaping Together in the Spirit

No one, regardless of ability or disability, answers God's call without power of the Holy Spirit who alone ignites obedience. Still, the question remains as to how people with intellectual disabilities can take a leap of obedience and participate in God's friendship. To be sure, any answers to questions about obedience and intellectual disability can only be conjecture, as the work of the Holy Spirit is, ultimately, a mystery. The Spirit moves how and where it will, always defying human logic and intellect. Even so, it may very well be that the Holy Spirit enables obedience in all people—those with and without intellectual disabilities—by working in and through authentic human relationships. Everyone must take their own leap of faith, but as beings created for relationship, no one can leap into faith by themselves. People necessarily—and by design—leap together.

People do not leap into faithfulness by themselves because people cannot be fully human by themselves. Human beings are fundamentally relational and are not truly human apart from relationships with other human beings.[30] At its core, humanity is co-humanity: a relationship, created in the image of a fundamentally relational God.[31] Though one in Godself, God is understood as Father, Son, and Holy Spirit and revealed most explicitly in the person of Jesus Christ.[32] In Christ, human beings see a reflection of the eternal relationship within the Godhead, which is the relationship after which human-ity is patterned. Jesus is also the means by which God demonstrates God's loving desire to be in relationship with all of God's children. In his fullness, Jesus is the very being of God, and his life constitutes God's gracious act of deliverance for all humankind.[33] Through his life, death, and resurrection, Jesus Christ enables human beings in every time and place to participate in a relationship with God that is analogous to the divine relationship between the Father and the Son.[34] Since all human beings were created in the relational image of God, as reflected in Jesus, all human beings reflect the nature of God in their existence with one another.[35]

God created human beings to be interrelated, committed to one another in mutually giving and caring relationships just as Christ was committed to his fellow human beings.[36] The basic form of humanity, then, is co-humanity, patterned after the very co-humanity of God as revealed in the person of Jesus Christ. People with intellectual and developmental disabilities are not classified as human according to a different standard simply because their cognitive and communicative challenges may require that they find creative ways to participate in authentic relationships. Their unique humanity must be allowed to flourish for its own sake and for the sake of others. While every person is always a being-in-encounter, no one person's individuality is sub-sumed or obscured by the presence or individuality of another. Every person remains a distinct, intact individual even as he or she encoun-ters others, and the preservation of each person's individuality is essen-tial to preserving the integrity of their encounter.[37] At the same time, while co-humanity thrives on authentic individuality, it fails when either being in an encounter insists on absolute self-sufficiency. No one can truly be himself or herself in isolation. People need one another in order to be fully human; in one person's encounter with another, each person's individual humanity is confirmed.[38] Since human beings need one another in order to be fully human, human beings need one another as they each take the "leap" of faith required to answer God's call to a life of discipleship.

Everyone answers God's call in the context of their co-humanity, and the encounter that is the foundation of co-humanity shapes each person's response to God. Yet when co-humanity includes intellectual disability, the very idea of an essential robust encounter as the foundation of authentic humanity raises questions, if not suspicions. However, when the notion of encounter is reimagined from the perspective of disability, people with and without intellectual disabilities can be acknowledged as partners together in encounter, in faith, and in vocation.[39] An encounter that fulfills basic human co-humanity involves meaningful interaction between two people, but meaningful interaction does not demand a particular degree of cognitive ability.

An authentic human encounter begins with purposive mutual recognition: two people who not only see each other but who are willing to be seen. Mutual recognition does not simply refer to the acknowledgment of another warm body. While physical eyesight can facilitate the acts of seeing and being seen, it is not essential, and it certainly cannot guarantee that two persons' encounter with one another will move beyond mere acknowledgment. More than physical acknowledgment alone, mutual recognition requires a posture of openness and a willingness to know and be known.[40] When people agree to see each other truly and to allow themselves to be seen, they welcome each other into their respective lives and, in so doing, agree to share their true selves with each other.

Once people agree to know each other and be known, their encounter can deepen through mutual communication. Authentic relationships are marked by mutually open, honest, and intentional communication. This kind of communication prevents either person in the relationship from making assumptions about the other and mitigates the kind of misunderstanding that can arise when true communication is lacking.[41] Just as eyes are not essential to mutual recognition in relationships, the mouth and ears can facilitate mutual communication but are not essential to it. Seeing is more than an activity of the eye, and communication involves more than the "normal" physical functioning of the ears and mouth.[42] Communication involves moving beyond mutual recognition and actually making oneself truly known to the other. Communication may also involve—and even require—moving beyond the physical acts of speaking and hearing in order for people to come to truly know one another. Relationships in which one or more people live with intellectual and developmental disabilities often thrive by means of alternative forms of communication. Some people may communicate through art—perhaps by painting or drawing a picture. Others may, out of necessity, communicate by using electronic communication devices or even simple images on a flip chart. Through improvisation and creativity, people with and without intellectual disabilities can communicate their true selves to each other and experience true relationship.

Every person's humanity is contingent upon his or her willingness to share himself or herself with another, as well as the other person's willingness to share, regardless of the challenges and risks that come with openness.[43] True relationship and authentic co-humanity require mutual transparency and vulnerability. These two qualities are not, however, always easy to embrace when intellectual disability informs the relationship. One or both people in the relationship may resist working toward the mutual communication necessary for authentic encounter—and with good reason. People with intellectual disabilities are often all too familiar with being misunderstood or ignored, even as they expend extraordinary amounts of energy to share their thoughts and feelings with others. Often, and tragically, resignation and introversion represent the path of least resistance for people with intellectual disabilities as they interact with others. Similarly, typically functioning individuals seeking meaningful communication with people with intellectual disabilities may find themselves either at a loss for words as they try to make meaningful connections in developmentally appropriate ways or too verbose as they try to fill the silence that may permeate the interaction. Authentic mutual communication can be a challenge for people with and without intellectual disabilities, yet the consequences of sidestepping genuinely mutual communication are significant. When people cannot or do not engage in authentic mutual communication, they are incapable of living into their own true humanity and they are incapable of recognizing the true humanity of others.[44]

Authentic mutual engagement in relationship inspires mutual concern and action. A lack of mutual recognition and communication in relationship breeds disinterest and inertia. On the other hand, people who have formed robust, authentic relationships with one another are not only willing but also eager to pour their mutual affection for one another into concrete acts of companionship, care, and assistance.[45] A robust, authentic relationship marked by mutual recognition, communication, and assistance in the living of everyday life is also marked by a spirit of gladness. Gladness is the deep gratification that accompanies people's awareness that they are living life with integrity because they are living life together. Gladness abounds when people embrace their co-humanity and therefore embrace one another as indispensable elements of their existence.[46] People cannot help but be glad when they realize that, in Jesus Christ, God has revealed that human beings are hardwired for relationships—with God and with one another.[47] There is no ambivalence or reluctance in authentic co-humanity. As people recognize one another, come to know one another, and assist one another in the living of life, they experience the gladness that only comes from claiming the God-given freedom of co-humanity—of life lived together in true fellowship.[48] With gladness shaping co-humanity, the act of leaping together into faithfulness to God's calling is not simply inevitable. It is, instead, a gift that all of God's children have the freedom to embrace.

Spirit-filled Co-humanity: The Locus of Obedience

The idea of leaping together in faith bodes well for all people. While each person bears the responsibility to commit to faithfulness, individual faith commitments are always made in the company of others. The idea of leaping together in faith is especially promising for people with intellectual disabilities who are often thought to be exempt from having responsibility before God or, worse, are seen as incapable of accepting whatever responsibility they might otherwise have. Despite the possibilities that the concept of co-humanity seems to hold for people with intellectual disabilities, questions remain regarding the realistic scope of its potential. Individuals with profound intellectual disabilities who function cognitively at little more than a sensory level may seem incapable of recognizing and knowing others and certainly seem incapable of offering help to anyone. If people with profound intellectual disabilities cannot assume a posture of mutuality in relationships with others—at least, not in a visible, tangible way—then perhaps a theological anthropology that posits a notion of co-humanity inevitably excludes people with profound intellectual disabilities.[49]

If intrinsic human rationality is a prerequisite for relationship, then people with intellectual disabilities are, to varying degrees, incapable of co-humanity. If, on the other hand, co-humanity is grounded extrinsically; that is, if it is grounded in something outside humanity, then a relational notion of *imago Dei* (co-humanity) eradicates distinctions between persons with and without disabilities and thus make space for people with even the most profound intellectual disabilities to be fully human.[50]

Since human beings have been created by a fundamentally relational God and in the image of that same relational God, human co-humanity is grounded in God—not in human beings. The soul is the enlivening, animating force of the human life and is inextricably linked to the body it inhabits.[51] Body and soul cannot live without each other, because a human being is "a soul of his body"—a life that belongs to the world of space and time.[52] Soul and body are interconnected, yet they are also unique components of the human being with unique operations that cannot be confused. The body serves the soul, and the soul guides the actions of the body.[53] Human beings, at once souls and bodies, live, move, and have their being because of the work of God that is enacted by the Holy Spirit.[54] Since the Holy Spirit enables the living of every human life, the Holy Spirit also enables the freedom with which *all* human beings are able to live authentically in encounter with one another.[55] The Spirit enables humans to recognize one another, regardless of the physical limitations of their senses, and facilitates communication, regardless of difficulties in speech and hearing. Even when physical mobility is compromised, the Spirit empowers mutual assistance and care. And the Spirit makes way for gladness in encounter, even in moments when fear and reluctance might otherwise prevail.

The Holy Spirit is vibrant and active in every human life, freeing everyone to be in true relationship with one another despite the challenges that intellectual disability might otherwise present. By the power of the Holy Spirit, intellectual disability is not a barrier to authentic encounter or to co-humanity.[56] Through the Holy Spirit, God seeks out God's children to be God's friends, fills the space between one person and another, and enables a co-humanity that is patterned after the very life of God. And by the power of the Holy Spirit, people with and without intellectual disabilities can partner together and say "Yes!" to the God who has called them to participate in God's friendship. Responding to God might involve one partner loaning the other partner his or her hands or voice in order to write or articulate prayers to God. Or responding to God might involve two or more people sitting together in sacred stillness, intentionally basking in the presence of God. And certainly, responding to God can take the form of people partnering together in a pastoral friendship and working together to discern God's great hopes and dreams for their lives.

DISCOVERING VOCATION THROUGH PASTORAL FRIENDSHIP

Through the power of the Holy Spirit, the agape-love with which God loves God's children also guides human relationships with others and enables each person in the relationship to fully experience the co-humanity that God intends.[57] Agape is a self-giving love in which the lover loves without expecting any reciprocity or even a gesture of gratitude from the beloved. Unlike erotic love, which is motivated by an expectation of personal benefit, agape-love is offered purely for the sake of the beloved and nothing more.[58] Through the power of the Holy Spirit, people can love one another with God's love, joining together in friendships marked by each friend offering what they have to the friendship without concern for what the other will offer in return.[59] In friendships marked by agape, there is no record keeping—no measurement or evaluation of the caliber of gifts offered from one friend to another. People with even the most profound intellectual disabilities can be genuine participants in agape friendships. The love that abides between them and their beloved is the product of the creative, transformative power of the Holy Spirit who disables the disabled/nondisabled dichotomies that might otherwise threaten the integrity of their friendship.[60]

When God's people engage friendships with one another as God intends, their human friendships reflect the love and friendship of God. In fact, friendships with God and with one another are inextricably linked, for it is through these loving friendships with one another that people can come to know God.[61] Friendships shaped by God's friendship and love can be transformative and empowering for all of God's people and, perhaps, especially for those with intellectual disabilities. When people with intellectual disabilities are able to participate in authentic, loving relationships, they not only experience and know something of God's love but also become participants in it.[62] Through the power of the Holy Spirit, friendship with God and fellow human beings can flourish, regardless of anyone's cognitive strengths or challenges.[63]

In the field of disability services and supports, friendship is an essential component of person-centered thinking and planning. In person-centered support, a person with disabilities partners with his or her closest circle of friends and support personnel to find ways to actualize the essence of his or her dreams. Pastoral care shaped by person-centered practices is also marked by mutuality, reciprocity, and friendship. The basic form of person-centered pastoral care, then, is a pastoral friendship: a collaborative relationship grounded in God's love.

The collaborative work between the caregiver and care receiver in a pastoral friendship is situated within and shaped by God's friendship. Through the power of the Holy Spirit, caregiver and care receiver can participate in an authentic friendship with one another—a friendship that reflects the love of the God who makes friendship possible.[64] In a pastoral friendship, the caregiver and care receiver creatively explore the care receiver's life, including needs, challenges, and dreams, in ways that are most appropriate for the care receiver. Through this loving, Spirit-driven collaboration, the care receiver is able to participate in God's friendship, which is nothing less than God's dream for his or her life. In their collaborative exploration of the care receiver's gifts, interests, and dreams, pastoral friends can explore ways in which the care receiver might employ his or her gifts, interests, and dreams in service to God. Consider, for example, a young man who has discerned that he has the spiritual gift of prophecy and who is passionate about prayer but, for reasons beyond his control, is unable to participate actively in a faith community. Together with his pastoral caregiver and friend, the young man might decide to cultivate his own vibrant prayer ministry from within the confines of his group home as a way of bearing witness to God's love and grace. Or, perhaps, consider a young woman who aspires to become both a successful model and a published poet and who also wants to find ways to serve and tell others about God. Through creative conversations with her pastoral friend, the young woman might decide to share her photo shoots and newly published poetry with others as a way to bear witness to the inherent beauty of all people, as well as to the many ways God employs women and men with disabilities in God's kingdom work. When a caregiver and care receiver partner together in a pastoral friendship to creatively discern God's dreams for their lives, nothing is impossible. Through the presence and power of the Holy Spirit, the God of impossible possibilities is leading their way.

Scripture tells the story of the Day of Pentecost, when the Holy Spirit sweeps through a culturally and linguistically diverse crowd of people and enables them to understand one another. In response to everyone's amazement, Peter reminds them of the words of the prophet Joel, through whom God said, "I will pour out my Spirit upon all flesh, and your sons and your daughters shall prophesy, and your young men shall see visions, and your old men shall dream dreams" (Acts 2:1-17). Indeed, God's Spirit has been poured out on all flesh, including flesh that is shaped, in part, by intellectual disability. Far too often, the sacred value and giftedness of people with intellectual disabilities are ignored—even by people who profess belief in the God responsible for the Spirit's outpouring. Person-centered pastoral care, enacted through pastoral friendships, bears witness to the miraculous work of the Spirit in the lives of all people, including people with intellectual disabilities. The witness of person-centered pastoral care takes the form of a caregiver—a pastoral friend—nurturing a sacred space wherein care receivers can, through the power of the Spirit, awaken to God's call to friendship and participate in it. Each person's vocation—the particular shape of his or her friendship with God—will be unique and can be explored creatively in the safe, nurturing, sacred space that the pastoral friendship affords. By the power of the Holy Spirit poured out on *all* flesh, God's sons and daughters with intellectual disabilities have prophecies to share, and young and old alike have dreams to dream. By God's grace, Christ's church can claim this good news.

SUGGESTIONS FOR FURTHER READING

Reinders, Hans. *Receiving the Gift of Friendship: Profound Disability, Theological Anthropology, and Ethics*. Grand Rapids: Eerdmans, 2008.

Reynolds, Thomas. *Vulnerable Communion: A Theology of Disability and Hospitality*. Grand Rapids: Brazos, 2008.

Yong, Amos. *Theology and Down Syndrome: Reimagining Disability in Late Modernity*. Waco, Tex.: Baylor University Press, 2007.

4

Playing
Person-Centered Pastoral Care in Practice

Person-centered pastoral care is a ministry of authentic togetherness. In person-centered pastoral care, two or more people partner together in a collaborative journey toward healing, growth, and wholeness. Collaboration is the foundation of person-centered pastoral care; however, person-centered pastoral care is not simply a working relationship between two people committed to a singular goal. At its best, person-centered pastoral care is a friendship—a holy relationship between two friends, the foundation of which is God's gracious love that transcends ability and disability and empowers discipleship in every human life.

The marks of a holy, person-centered friendship are mutual closeness, communication, and deep listening to each other's thoughts and needs, all of which are facilitated by God's Holy Spirit who is alive and active within the friendship.[1] Friends engaged in collaborative, person-centered pastoral care are willing to sit close together. Person-centered friends sit close enough to each other that they truly know each other and are grateful for the opportunity to work together as partners in support and in action. To be sure, partners in person-centered care cannot meet every need or solve every problem. What a person-centered caregiver can do, however, is listen carefully to a care receiver's hopes and dreams and explore the ways these hopes and dreams can shape the care receiver's life. One important component of the deep listening that transpires in a pastoral friendship is an ability to tease out the different kinds of issues that often lie beneath the surface of a conversation so that the friend receiving care can be fully heard. A pastoral caregiver can give more thorough attention to every aspect of a care receiver's needs, hopes, and dreams when the caregiver can identify and address spiritual and theological issues with the resources of faith, while also identifying and tending to emotional, social, and psychological issues with the resources of social science. Equipped with a variety of interpretive resources and guided by the Holy Spirit, pastoral friends can "play" with thoughts and ideas from a variety of disciplines as they discern together God's dreams for their lives.

THINKING IT THROUGH: AN INTERPRETIVE GUIDE

The organic, creative collaboration that happens in a person-centered pastoral care relationship is, by nature, complex. The conversations that transpire and the activities engaged in within the context of pastoral friendship are always multidimensional and can only be fully understood when the caregiver and care receiver consider their "play" from a variety of perspectives. In other words, person-centered pastoral friendships are fundamentally interdisciplinary. Pastoral care is an interdisciplinary practice necessarily reliant on insights from both theological and social scientific disciplines. Pastoral care is also a ministry, an act of faithfulness to God. Christian pastoral care, then, is an interdisciplinary ministry of the church and an act of faithfulness to the God who is revealed in Jesus Christ.

Given the complex characteristics that fund pastoral care's distinctiveness as a Christian practice, it is helpful for person-centered pastoral caregivers to approach their ministry with some sort of guide for interpreting their conversations with care receivers. The complex concerns or issues that care receivers bring to the pastoral friendship are best met with careful listening and multidimensional interpretation that draws from various disciplines—most often theology and psychology. At the same time, as pastoral caregivers engage in careful listening and interpretation with care receivers, they must bear in mind that, first and foremost, they are engaging in a practice of ministry.[2] This fundamental aspect of pastoral friendship sets the terms by which a caregiver utilizes resources in practices of care. Clarity about the relationship between and use of psychology and theology in pastoral care equips the pastoral caregiver to use the resources of these disciplines in ways that are both appropriate for the specific needs of the care receiver and reflective of the caregiver's vocational commitments.

Chaplains in institutional settings typically provide spiritual and emotional support to staff and clients from a variety of faith traditions, both Christian and non-Christian. However, Christian chaplains have been trained for and ordained to ministry in Christ's church, even when they are serving outside the bounds of a local faith community. Likewise, pastoral care is a ministry of the church, even when care-givers are working with people who either have faith commitments that are different from those of the caregivers or people who cannot articulate a faith commitment at all.

There is no specific formula for using theological and social sci-entific resources in pastoral care. After all, pastoral care is an art—a creative encounter between a caregiver and care receiver. Because pas-toral care is an art, it takes different shapes with each pastoral relation-ship. Even so, interpretive guides such as the Chalcedonian approach facilitate the caregiver's thinking and practice and shape the "play" within the pastoral friendship. According to the Chalcedonian defini-tion, Christ's divine and human natures are inextricably connected yet remain separate and distinct natures even as they commingle within Christ's person.[3] Furthermore, Christ's two natures exist in an asym-metrical order. While both natures are essential, Christ's divine nature is logically prior to his human nature and provides the framework within which to understand and interpret His humanity.[4]

While the Chalcedonian *definition* is, exclusively, a substantive statement about the dual nature of Christ, a Chalcedonian *approach* to interpretation provides a pattern or formula by which to consider the relationship between terms and concepts, including social science and theology.[5] As pastoral caregivers listen to care receivers in the context of their pastoral friendship, caregivers recognize that the theological and psychological issues coexist and commingle in the care receiver's life. For example, even when a care receiver comes to the care relation-ship desiring to address a theological issue, the caregiver may sense that there are psychological issues informing the care receiver's theo-logical concern.[6] Even though psychological and theological issues do coexist, they are conceptually distinct and must be interpreted in distinct way. Psychology and theology are different disciplines with different methods of enquiry. Theological language and terminology cannot adequately explain psychological phenomena. Likewise, theological concepts cannot be explained psychologically. If caregivers confuse the methods and norms of the two disciplines when attempting to address a care receiver's needs and issues, they compromise their ability to address those needs and issues adequately.

Another aspect of the distinctiveness of theological and psychological issues is their conceptual asymmetry. At the theoretical level, theology functions on a different conceptual level than psychology, not only because the scope of theology is broader than that of psychology but also because the basis for theological thought is found in revelation and not in empirical or phenomenological analysis.[7] Interpretations of a pastoral care receiver's psychological issues are understood within the broader framework of theology. Practically speaking, this means that when pastoral caregivers offer care as a ministry of the church, the norms and values of faith become the framework within which psychological issues and needs are understood.[8] In person-centered pastoral care, caregivers and care receivers "play" together with ideas from psychology or other scientific disciplines. Their explorations of issues and needs take place within the holy space of their pastoral friendship, which is patterned after the very life and friendship of God and revealed in Jesus Christ.

PRACTICING PERSON-CENTERED CARE

Person-centered pastoral friendships involve careful attention to the needs of care receivers and collaboration with care receivers to address those needs. In some cases, the issues at "play" will be both theological and psychological. In other cases, the "bilingual" pastoral caregiver will only need to use the resources of one of these disciplines to address the needs at hand. In every case, the pastoral caregiver engaged in this collaborative work bears witness, however implicitly or explicitly, to the fact that all people have been called to friendship with God and that something of this friendship can be known in pastoral friendships.[9]

The following excerpts from actual pastoral care conversations are taken from a chaplain's ministry at a facility for children and adults with developmental and intellectual disabilities.[10] Each conversation demonstrates the variety of ways in which pastoral caregivers and care receivers can collaborate in holy, creative, person-centered friendships. None of these three care receivers come to the chaplain with a desire to talk specifically about God. Furthermore, the chaplain does not try to force a theological conversation upon any of the residents simply because she is their chaplain. The conversations between the chaplain and the care receivers focus mainly on social, emotional, or psychological issues in the care receivers' lives. Nevertheless, the theological commitments undergirding the chaplain's identity as a Christian minister provide the framework within which to interpret the "play" in her pastoral friendships with these care receivers, even though she does not deal specifically with the care receivers' relationships with God.

Coloring with Bill

Bill is a thirty-one-year-old male whose cognitive functioning might best be equated with that of a very young typically functioning child. He uses a manual wheelchair to get around and is able to operate it on his own. He also has limited use of both of his hands. Bill enjoys roaming the halls of the facility where he lives (often in lieu of attending classes in the adult day program), watching people come and go, and greeting his friends. Bill is very solicitous of other people's time and attention; he often sees the chaplain across a room, points his finger, and says, "Hey! You! I want to talk to you!" For Bill, though, "talking" has more to do with time spent together than it does with actual conversation. He is not very talkative—at least, not with the chaplain—yet he is always eager to find a time to meet with her.

Early in the chaplain's ministry, she plans and promotes an evening Bible study and garners a good bit of interest from several residents at the facility. Bill has not expressed interest, but he and the chaplain have become friends, and when he sees her heading to the Bible study, he goes with her. Unbeknownst to the chaplain, another event is taking place concurrently (and in another building), and all the residents who had previously said they wanted to come to the study have gone to the other event instead. The chaplain is disappointed. No one comes to her Bible study—no one except for Bill.

Bill has at least a minimal awareness of the chaplain's roll at the facility, and while he never expresses a desire to talk explicitly about God, he always wants to talk to the chaplain. Unlike many of her colleagues, whose professions demand that they balance direct patient care with committee meetings and mountains of paperwork, the chaplain's primary (and really only) responsibility is to spend time with residents. Bill knows the chaplain is there for him. Furthermore, the chaplain knows that Bill's greatest need in that moment is to be in the presence of someone "whose only responsibility [is] to be in his presence."[11] Nevertheless, the chaplain does not presume that Bill does not care that she is a minister. In fact, in their early one-on-one conversations, the chaplain makes extra efforts to "do her job"—that is, to cultivate a quality pastoral conversation by finding out about him through a line of questioning that is perilously akin to the game "Twenty Questions." To most, if not all, of the chaplain's questions, Bill replies, "I don't know." Before long, the chaplain realizes that her relationship with Bill needs to be shaped by something other than questions and answers. As it turns out, friendship provides the perfect context, and coloring together—one of Bill's favorite pastimes—emerges as the perfect medium.

On the evening of the pastoral conversation recounted here, Bill and the chaplain wait in a classroom for other Bible study participants to arrive. In typical fashion, Bill is calm while he waits, clearly content to "go with the flow." After approximately ten minutes, the chaplain leaves the room to inquire at a nearby nurses' station about the whereabouts of other potential participants. Upon learning that everyone else has gone to a program in another building, the disappointed chaplain returns to the classroom, looks at Bill, and says, "Well, Bill, I guess it's just you and me." Bill replies with a simple, "Okay." After all, his goal is to spend time with the chaplain. He does not seem to care what form the visit takes—until the chaplain mentions having paper and markers in her bag. At this point, he became unusually animated and very eager to find a place where he and the chaplain can color together. Bill and the chaplain move to a conference room down the hall. The room has a large table in its center, and is more conducive to coloring than a classroom. Once Bill finds his place at the conference room table and wheels himself to it, his sense of calm returns. The chaplain sits in a chair next to Bill, pulls several pieces of paper out of her bag, gives one to Bill, and keeps one for herself. Next, she pulls out a bag of markers and asks Bill which color he would like to use. He chooses purple—his favorite color. The chaplain takes the cap off the marker and places the marker in Bill's right hand. For the next fifteen to twenty minutes, Bill and the chaplain sit in silence and color. Occasionally, Bill looks over at the chaplain's paper, smiles, and resumes his own coloring. Very little is said for the next fifteen minutes until it is time to conclude the meeting. The chaplain gently tells Bill that the time has come for them to say goodbye for the evening, and she asks Bill if he would like her to put his drawing in the backpack on the back of his wheelchair. He says no and tells the chaplain that he wants her to keep his drawing. The chaplain thanks Bill and helps him sign his name to his drawing—just as all artists do. She tells Bill that she will be back in a few days and will see him then. He agrees and says goodbye.

Given his unusually animated positive response to the chaplain's invitation to sit in a room together and color, it appears that Bill simply needs an opportunity to *play*. He needs a safe, unchallenged space where he can rest and relax as he plays without having to make sense of it.[12] Bill needs to play in a manner different from how he plays during other parts of his weekly routine. Like many residents and day program participants at the facility where he lives, Bill participates in an arts program in which professional artists (painters, sculptors, dancers, and writers) literally "loan" program participants their hands so that the participants can create works of art. For example, a participant wishing to paint a picture will tell the professional artist exactly what colors of paints to use, what brushes or other utensils to use to apply the paint, and what sort of strokes to make on the canvas. Bill's participation in the arts program is likely a source of empowerment for him, not to mention a means of making a contribution to his community. Participation in the arts program is also a form of play, through which Bill can discover and connect with his deepest, most authentic self in ways that are not always possible with words.

While the interaction between the facilitators and participants in Bill's facility's arts program is a partnership (and has to be), the facilitators intentionally try to remove themselves (their own tastes, perspectives, opinions, and biases) from the interaction so that the art that emerges from their collaboration is purely the work of the participant. The program's approach to art is essential to the success of the program and the authenticity of the participants' artistic creations. However, the relationship between Bill and the chaplain is entirely—and necessarily—different. In their time together, Bill does not want the chaplain simply to step away and allow him to color, nor does he want the chaplain simply to sit, watch him color, and ask him questions about his art's meaning. Rather, he wants the chaplain to create something of her own while he creates something of his own. Bill wants the chaplain to contribute something to the relationship and to this particular interaction. By joining Bill in his creative endeavor, the chaplain enables Bill to receive what he most needed to receive during their time together: a sense of true companionship. Similarly, by accepting Bill's artistic creation as the gift he intends it to be, the chaplain both acknowledges and claims Bill's participation in a relationship that is different from that of an artist and facilitator.

Bill needs his time with the chaplain to be different from the time he spends with the arts program facilitators, as well as the time he spent with other employees at the facility. Many of Bill's conversations withstaff are driven by agendas—and necessarily so. Social workers, therapists, personal care attendants, nurses, and doctors all have specific issues and topics to address when they meet with Bill. In the chaplain's conversation with Bill, she functioned as more of a collaborator and partner than a purveyor of goods and services.[13] The sense of calm Bill regains when he and the chaplain move their meeting from a classroom to a room more conducive to coloring reflects Bill's deep need for a different kind of interaction. In both a literal and a figurative sense, Bill wants his time with the chaplain to fill a different space—his own space. In the course of their visit, the chaplain followed Bill's lead, allowing him to establish the rules of their play instead of assuming either that she knew how the play should be done or that she knew better than Bill what he needed in that moment. The rules—Bill's rules—involved coloring together in silence. By nurturing Bill's particular style of play, the chaplain was not simply a service provider. She was Bill's collaborator and friend.[14]

From a psychological perspective, the chaplain's presence with Bill functions as participation in his experience of play. The only toys needed in their play are markers and paper. As soon as the chaplain mentions having coloring supplies in her bag and sees Bill's reaction to hearing this information, the chaplain realizes that she has made a good choice in abandoning her original plans for a more traditional Bible study. Bill wants to sit with the chaplain and color. The chaplain believes that it is more important to follow Bill's needs than her original plan which, in actuality, had been made without Bill in mind (given his previous lack of participation in Bible studies). In scripture, Jesus instructs his disciples to feed his sheep. While sheep instinctively have a group mentality, no two sheep are identical, but all are in need of nourishment that will truly satisfy. Jesus' disciples are called to feed the sheep in their midst, nourishing them with the sustenance that will meet the particular sheep's individual needs.[15] Through collaborative play, Bill is able to express himself in ways that make sense to him. The chaplain, as Bill's collaborator, does not try to make sense out of what others might call Bill's nonsense. Instead, the chaplain affirms Bill's need to rest, to relax, and to simply *be*. In so doing, the chaplain demonstrates to Bill that all communication—and all of his communication—is meaningful.

When Bill indicates to the chaplain that he wants to sit in a different room and color, he is asking for a different kind of activity than the chaplain originally had in mind when she scheduled her evening group activity. Bill wants to color with his chaplain and, in so doing, enjoy the kind of friendship and community that are deeply important to him. From a theological perspective, Bill needs to give and receive the gift of hospitality; he needs to be welcomed into a safe, comfortable space. Bill needs to be cared for in a manner that reflects *his* needs—not his caregiver's expectations. At the same time, he needs to be able to welcome the chaplain as a friend willing to participate in a relationship of creative expression.

Once the chaplain relinquishes her own preconceptions of what a pastoral conversation "ought" to look like and focuses on Bill's particular needs, she is able to participate with him in an act of true hospitality. Hospitality involves careful, intentional listening to the needs of others, a willingness to share oneself authentically with another, and a willingness to share time and resources generously with another.[16] Hospitality shaped by Christ reflects the co-humanity that is the truest and most basic form of humanity. Co-humanity requires the mutual seeing, speaking, listening, helping, and acting with gladness that make us fully human. In her conversation with Bill, the chaplain cannot be a distant host who, after securing all necessary provisions, simply sits and watches while Bill, the guest, makes lines on a page with a purple marker. Hospitality is reflected in and nurtured by friendship, in which guest and host alike are free to welcome each other. Through this kind of mutual welcome, Bill and the chaplain are able to connect with each other in a virtually wordless conversation. The chaplain welcomes Bill into a safe, comfortable space where he can simply *be*, and Bill invites the chaplain to participate with him in his act of self-expression. In their pastoral friendship, each of these individuals is both guest and host.

Through shared practices of hospitality, Bill and the chaplain are able to connect with who they really are: people of God who have been created and called to be God's friends. In the context of their pastoral friendship, the hospitality that Bill and the chaplain extend to each other is not of their own making. Their acts of hospitality are part and parcel of God's much greater hospitality toward all of God's children.[17] The pastoral friendship between Bill and the chaplain does not simply *reflect* God's love and friendship. Rather, their friendship is possible because God has first loved and befriended each of them. Furthermore, it is God's work through the Holy Spirit that makes possible the friendship between Bill and the chaplain, despite the challenges to communication that Bill's disability might otherwise present.

The chaplain's person-centered pastoral care with Bill does not involve an in-depth exchange of ideas or an explicit identification of needs and wants. Instead, it involves the chaplain's willingness simply to be present and collaborate with him in ways that are comfortable and appropriate for him. By participating in this collaboration, the chaplain not only respects and meets Bill's needs for acceptance and companionship but also honors the fact that friendship is important to him. Over the next several years, the pastoral friendship between Bill and the chaplain takes the same shape as the encounter just described. On most occasions, the chaplain supplies the paper and markers. On some occasions, however, Bill insists on providing the necessary supplies. Often, at the close of their conversations, Bill gives his artwork to the chaplain. On other occasions, he offers his artwork as a gift to someone else. Through his creative collaboration with the chaplain, Bill is able to participate in a true friendship in which he is both a giver and a receiver. In so doing, Bill is able to live fully into his God-given co-humanity.

Writing Poetry with Jerry

Jerry is in his late twenties and has a developmental disability that includes intellectual disability. Jerry uses a wheelchair to get from one place to another in the facility where he lives. Jerry's chair is not motorized, and he must rely on others to get him where he needs to go. Some of the symptoms of Jerry's disability render him unable to operate a wheelchair on his own. These same symptoms make his speech difficult for many people to understand and also prevent him from being able to use his hands to write. Even so, he enjoys writing letters and poems to his girlfriend with the help of support providers—including the chaplain—who serve as his scribes. Like many of his peers at the facility, Jerry yearns to have an intimate romantic relationship with another person. He does his best to cultivate romantic relationships, despite the enormous challenges that his disability brings. Among these challenges is the reality that most of his activities and communication with women at the facility are necessarily mediated by support staff. Nevertheless, Jerry perseveres.

Jerry's disability is not the only factor compromising his success in relationships with women. Jerry is very volatile, and this volatility is most frequently demonstrated by his fiery temper. He often loses his temper when he is eating meals with fellow residents in the dining hall. One of the more frequent recipients of his wrath is his on-again, off-again girlfriend, Emily. Emily is a young female resident who tends to be unkind to Jerry and seems to enjoy making him jealous. One day after Jerry and Emily have another argument, Jerry calls out to the chaplain as she is walking down the hallway and asks her to meet with him. Once again, Jerry has ended his relationship with Emily.

The chaplain has known Jerry for at least a year and has already had enough interaction with him to develop a fairly strong rapport. She has also gotten rather adept at understanding his speech, which strengthens the quality of her conversations with Jerry and gives Jerry a greater sense of ease (he gets noticeably frustrated when people trying to help him are unable to understand his speech). Jerry usually sees the chaplain as a person who, like his social worker, is frequently available to listen to him as he explores his particular needs and concerns. Jerry understands that the chaplain is a minister, but he does not always wish to have an explicitly spiritual conversation with her. Occasionally, when Jerry meets with the chaplain, Jerry will ask questions about God and will sometimes ask to pray. These explicitly spiritual conversations often occur around significant holidays when Jerry experiences a heightened level of grief over the deaths of loved ones. Often, these conversations include at least a brief mention of his disability and his curiosity about God's reasons for letting him be born with a disability. In most cases, however, the chaplain's conversations with Jerry are not spiritual or theological in nature—at least not overtly so.

On the occasion of this particular visit, the chaplain is not sure what Jerry wants to talk about, though she suspects that he might have some concerns regarding his girlfriend, Emily. Given the intermittent nature of their relationship, this is a common topic of conversation for Jerry, not only with the chaplain but also with his social worker and his other direct support providers. Still, the chaplain approaches the conversation in a spirit of openness and without any preconceptions about what Jerry will say—or what she will or will not say in response.

When the time of their meeting arrives, the chaplain finds Jerry and wheels him down the hall to the conference room. As they settle into the conference room to begin their conversation, Jerry's demeanor reflects frustration. His frustration is most evident in his eyes, which are very expressive, and in the spastic movements of his body, which are more pronounced during times of anxiety and frustration. When the chaplain asks Jerry how he is doing, he communicates with both his demeanor and his words that he is "not good." He explains that, on the previous evening, he "cussed out" his girlfriend because she cheated on him with someone else. He then says that he and Emily have once again ended their relationship. The chaplain conveys her sympathy to Jerry and validates his desire to end the relationship because of Emily's infidelity. When Jerry explains that he is heartbroken and unsure of what to do now, the chaplain draws on Jerry's gifts as an artist to try to comfort him. The chaplain reminds Jerry that artists use their artwork to help them through difficult times. When she mentions that poets often write poetry to find solace, Jerry interrupts her and immediately asks if she has paper and a pencil. He tells the chaplain that he wants to write Emily a poem to tell her how he feels.

Once again, Jerry asks the chaplain to be his scribe and to help him write a message to the woman who has broken his heart. The chaplain readies her pen and paper and invites Jerry to begin dictating his poem. She writes down every word that he speaks:

> I have a lot going on for me.
> I am funny.
> I am handsome.
> I have a lot of friends.

The remainder of Jerry's poem is similar to many of the letters he has written to Emily. He tells her of his love for her and his sadness over her unfaithfulness. Struck by the message contained in the first four lines of Jerry's poem, the chaplain believes that these lines reflect the issues that Jerry really needs to address. After Jerry completes his poem, the chaplain comments on the power of his first four lines, in which he acknowledges his own gifts and strengths. She points out to Jerry that in these four lines, he is not only telling Emily that he is special, he is telling himself that he is special, too. In response to the chaplain's observation, Jerry asks the chaplain to read his poem's first four lines over and over again. What is intended as a message to Emily becomes a vehicle of support and hope for Jerry as he struggles with a significant yet turbulent relationship and its impact on his self-image.

The rest of Jerry's conversation with the chaplain focuses on Jerry's temper, how it compromises his relationships, and how he might try to control it in the future. Being the poet that he is, Jerry calls his temper a "volcano" and, together with the chaplain, describes moments .in which his temper "erupts" and his words, like lava, spew out and create a mess in his relationships with others. The chaplain invites

Jerry to brainstorm some ways he can tame the "volcano" when he senses that it is about to erupt. Together, Jerry and the chaplain come up with strategies that Jerry can use to avoid angry outbursts, including listening to music on his iPod and simply asking his personal care attendant to move him away from someone (especially Emily) who is irritating or provoking him. After spending approximately thirty minutes together, Jerry and the chaplain end their conversation. The chaplain encourages Jerry to memorize the first four lines of his poem to Emily and to say them over and over again to himself. He assures her that he will.

Jerry's choice of the volcano as an image to describe himself is perfect. Like natural volcanoes, Jerry has moments when he is dormant. He is kind, playful, and fun-loving. At other times, he is truly explosive, as his temper gets the better of him and "erupts." Jerry is often able to control his temper. However, the complexities of his disability often prevent him from having control over his temper—or anything else, for that matter. Jerry has little to no control of his body and must therefore rely on others in order to meet virtually all his needs. Jerry's lack of control over so many aspects of his daily life fuels his anger and frustration, making it all the more difficult for him to keep his temper at bay.

The most significant psychological issue that Jerry and the chaplain face in their play is Jerry's anger and the threat that it poses to his sense of self, his significant relationships, and his future hopes and dreams. Anger is threatening, not only to people who are the recipients of a person's anger but also to the angry person himself. Anger can be triggered by physical threats—things that put physical health and well-being in danger—and, more frequently, by psychological threats—things that are perceived as threats to a person's values and expectations.[18] To be sure, Jerry's medically complex developmental disability is a physical threat to him and, thus, a source of his anger. However, the greater sources of his anger are several psychological threats, some of which are related to his disability and some of which are not. First, Jerry's anger is a response to a threatened sense of self. Jerry wants to be a person who can control his anger, yet his disability and other factors often compromise his sense of control. When Jerry loses control of his temper, his self-esteem suffers, and his expectations of himself are threatened.[19] A second threat that ignites Jerry's anger is the threat to a significant relationship—namely, his relationship with Emily. Jerry depends heavily on his relationship with his fellow residents and staff people, and many of the behavioral components of his disability cause him to sabotage his relationships with others. Similarly, Jerry also depends on his relationship with Emily as a source of security and meaning in his life, which explains his willingness to try to "win her back" over and over again. Thus, her infidelity threatens Jerry's security and meaning, not to mention the happiness that he experiences as a result of participating in a significant relationship.[20] Jerry's anger threatens his relationship with his friends and his relationship with Emily.

This second threat that Jerry feels is closely tied to a third: the threat to his future hopes and dreams.[21] Jerry has long dreamed of marrying Emily and sharing a home with her. At one point, he even purchased an engagement ring for her as a symbol of his commitment to their shared future. The residents at Jerry's facility are not permitted to marry each other, and Jerry knows this.[22] Nevertheless, he dreams of spending his life together with Emily in whatever way he can—not unlike many other young men his age who anticipate finding a mate and building a life with that mate. However, Jerry's anger and Emily's chronic infidelity threaten these particular hopes and dreams. Jerry does not envision a future in solitude, yet his anger and the instability that it brings to his relationships present threats of alienation and isolation. Jerry does not want to be alone. He wants a life in which he is surrounded by family, friends, and a significant other who loves and respects him.

Jerry and the chaplain explore his anger and its consequences by "playing" with words. Words—and the images they help create—are the medium through which Jerry and the chaplain can work together to address and explore Jerry's needs.[23] First, they play with the words of the poem that he writes for Emily. The first four lines create an image that reflects Jerry's idealized self. His idealized self is the self that he wants Emily to know and to appreciate. Jerry asks the chaplain to repeat the first four lines of his poem over and over again, which suggests that Jerry needs to hear his own words for his own benefit.

Jerry's anger is likely compromising his ability to claim his own gifts and strengths.

After playing with the first lines of his poem, Jerry and the chaplain play with Jerry's image of a volcano. The image of the volcano helps Jerry and the chaplain think through the anger that often obscures Jerry's view of his best self and compromises his relationships with others. Jerry and the chaplain talk about how and when the volcano "erupts" and what might be done to stave off an eruption. Since Jerry's volcanic temper can sometimes be controlled, he and the chaplain work together to consider concrete strategies that Jerry might employ to control his temper and to keep it from wreaking havoc on his self-esteem and his relationships. By playing with the images that emerge through his poetry and his poetic imagination, Jerry is able to regain a sense of control over the way he lives his life—a life that he may feel he lives at the mercy of others. To be sure, the complex challenges of living with his disability persist, including his volatile temper and his difficulties in cultivating romantic relationships. However, in the pastoral playroom, Jerry's challenges no longer seemed to pose an insurmountable threat.

Theologically, there is nothing bad or wrong about Jerry's anger in and of itself. However, Jerry's inability to control his temper compromises his ability to sustain important relationships in his life, including his relationship with Emily, as well as his feelings of self-worth. The common assumption that anger itself is always sinful runs counter to messages found in Christian scripture.[24] Both the Old and New Testaments bear witness to the value of righteous anger, while at the same time encouraging God's people to refrain from letting anger become destructive.[25] Indeed, God calls God's children to handle their anger creatively, and that is exactly what Jerry and the chaplain do with Jerry's anger during their time together. Words and images become the tools with which Jerry is able to process his anger. Jerry's poem to Emily becomes a way for Jerry to address his anger toward her, while also asserting his own sense of self-worth. Jerry's discussion with the chaplain about the "volcano" provides a way to identify Jerry's capacity for anger as a part of God's good creation but also affords Jerry the opportunity to consider ways he can control the spewing "lava" (expression of anger).[26] The chaplain acknowledges that Jerry has a right to be angry and partners with him to explore more constructive ways of coping with his anger when it arises.

After discerning that Jerry is struggling with his self-worth as a result of his angry outburst, the chaplain asks to revisit the first four lines of Jerry's poem, in which he detailed his gifts and strengths. When the chaplain reads Jerry's words back to him, Jerry joyfully asks the chaplain to repeat the words several more times. It is as if he is hearing his words for the first time. Jerry needs to hear himself speak these words of affirmation, but he also needs to hear someone else speak his words back to him. Jerry needs to rediscover and embrace the mutuality that is essential to his true humanity (co-humanity). When Jerry lashes out at the people he loves most, he is alone, and lonely, and incomplete. He is not able to experience the gladness that comes from knowing that he, too, was created for community and fellowship with others. His inability to deal constructively with his anger compromises his fundamental, God-given co-humanity, as well as his ability to love both his neighbor and himself. By the power and presence of the Holy Spirit working through his creative collaboration with the chaplain, Jerry is able to regain mutuality and feel truly human again. To be sure, the specific words of Jerry's poem are a source of strength and affirmation for him. Yet the mutual hearing, listening, and speaking with the chaplain that bring his words to life are equally important to him, if not more so.

Over the course of the ensuing weeks and months, Jerry and the chaplain often revisit the subject of Emily. Jerry and Emily continue to have an intermittent relationship, and Jerry continues to lose his temper whenever he becomes aware of her interest in someone else. Occasionally, when he expresses disappointment in himself for losing his temper, the chaplain reminds him of the poem he wrote in this earlier meeting. One day, Jerry tells the chaplain that he has finally given Emily a piece of his mind—but in a calmer, more constructive way (in his words, only "a little bit of lava" this time). He has written Emily a letter in which he tells her that he does not appreciate the way that she treats him and that he will only agree to be her boyfriend if she agrees to treat him with love and respect. The chaplain congratulates Jerry on his successful interaction with Emily and tells him how proud she is of him. She reminds him that his successful interaction with Emily is truly a "big deal" and reflects a lot of hard work on his part. Throughout the rest of their brief conversation, Jerry asks the chaplain no less than three times, "Are you really proud of me?" The chaplain assures Jerry that she is truly proud of him. Similar to their earlier encounter in which Jerry needed to hear someone else utter his own words of self-affirmation, Jerry now needs to hear the chaplain's affirmation. He needs to be heard and affirmed with gladness. In short, he needs to experience the mutuality that comes through an authentic encounter between one person and another. In and through his pastoral friendship with the chaplain, his need is met.

Telling Secrets with RaRa

RaRa is a young woman in her early thirties whose mild intellectual disability is accompanied by a severely debilitating developmental disability.[27] She uses a wheelchair to move around the facility where she lives, but the nature of her disability prevents her from being able to operate it herself. She relies on others to take her where she wants to go. RaRa grieves her physical condition and the limits it places on her ability to enjoy life in the ways that are most important to her. While her grief is often visible and often a topic of conversation with her caregivers, RaRa still manages to enjoy life in as many ways as she can. She is often seen with fashion or pop culture magazines on her lap (with more in her wheelchair), and her iPod, full of the latest and best popular music, is either playing or ready to be played. RaRa is a snappy, "fashion-forward" dresser and changes her hairstyle frequently.

In general, RaRa loves many of the delicacies that life can offer. She loves music, art, culture, and fashion. She loves love, she loves children, and she loves family. Her own life, however, bears little resemblance to the life she wants to live. Two of RaRa's biggest dreams for her life are to get rid of her disability and to fall in love and get married (preferably to someone without a disability). She frequently develops "crushes" on young male staff members and grieves when she discovers that they are involved in romantic relationships of their own. This, of course, returns her to her pervasive grief about her own life and her inability to escape the challenges it brings. Aspects of RaRa's family system compound the sadness she feels when she considers the shape of her life. RaRa has two other siblings, one of whom is her twin sister who does not have a developmental disability. From the confines of an institution, RaRa watches her twin lead a "normal" life full of possibilities that RaRa's life can never have.

RaRa often seeks out the chaplain for support. Sometimes she talks to the chaplain about how much she hates life, and she often questions how her profound disabilities could possibly be part of God's plan. At other times, however, their conversations are not overtly spiritual—as in the case of the visit described here. On this day of this visit, the chaplain meets RaRa, who is sitting in the hallway outside her bedroom. RaRa immediately asks to spend some time with the chaplain. They decide to go to the children's dining room, which is largely unused when meals are not being served. RaRa and the chaplain choose a table. The chaplain positions RaRa's wheelchair at the table and sits in a chair next to her. On her lap she is holding an envelope and several blank postcards. When the chaplain asks RaRa how she is doing, RaRa replies by telling the chaplain the reason for their conversation. RaRa wants to write down her deepest secrets and send them to PostSecret, a sort of "secrets clearinghouse" that has recently gained popularity in the media. PostSecret was created in 2004 by Frank Warren and now includes both a website and mailing address where people can share their secrets.[28] RaRa needs the chaplain to write down her secrets and then mail them on her behalf. The chaplain agrees to help her.

RaRa begins naming the secrets that she wants to include in her mailing. She wants to find a cure for her disability. She wants to concoct a potion that will make someone fall in love with her. She wants to walk. She wants to get married and have children. RaRa continues naming secrets, all of which deal in some way with removing the barriers that her disability has placed in her life. The chaplain is struck by RaRa's definition of a secret, yet instead of offering what would be an unsolicited pastoral commentary, the chaplain simply continues writing RaRa's secrets on blank postcards. Once this task has been completed, RaRa asks the chaplain to take her back to her room. They say their goodbyes and, in typical fashion, RaRa blows the chaplain a kiss. Per RaRa's request, the chaplain mails the secrets in a plain manila envelope, using only the name of the institution in the return address.

RaRa's "secrets" are her hopes and dreams for her life. By sending them to PostSecret, she does what literally millions of other people have done since Frank Warren created the program in 2004: she gives a voice to her heart's deepest desires (implicit fears) in a safe, non-judgmental venue.[29] Furthermore, by naming her secrets and sending them to PostSecret (where they may in fact be published for the world to see), RaRa believes that her hopes and dreams can be validated without qualification. Were RaRa to share her particular secrets with one or more of her caregivers, they might offer her the gentle reminder that, to date, there is no cure for her disability. There is no such thing as a love potion. There is no way that she can walk on her own. Gentle reminders like these would never be offered in a spirit of unkindness but instead out of a loving desire to help RaRa make the most of her life as it is, rather than allowing her to spend her days fantasizing about what can never be. The chaplain, too, has had conversations with RaRa about the heartbreaking limitations that come with her disability. Honest conversations about RaRa's life are important and necessary. RaRa is well aware of what is possible and what is impossible when it comes to the concrete aspects of her life. Nevertheless, she finds herself dreaming of a different and better life but feels the need to keep her dreams hidden.

In psychological terms RaRa's identification of her hopes and dreams as "secrets" reflects her feelings of shame. RaRa does not feel like she has the right to have dreams of a better life, particularly since support personnel are frequently (and with good intentions) trying to redirect her thinking. RaRa's sense of shame causes her to perceive herself as fundamentally flawed and deficient as a human being. She cannot eliminate her disability, nor can she pretend that she does not want a different kind of life for herself. She is stuck.[30] She is caught in an identity crisis rooted in shame. She knows the particular challenges that come with her disability; she knows that she cannot do anything to "fix" her body. At the same time, the hopes and dreams she has for her life are not unlike those of many other young women her age. The limitations that her disability imposes—including limitations on physical mobility and the possibility of intimate sexual relationships—do not limit the desires of her heart.

Disability does not eliminate desires—or dreams. It seems as though she "knows better" than to dream these dreams for her life, yet she cannot help but do so. This "gap between her actions and the expectations of her environment" fuels her shameful feelings.[31] RaRa cares deeply about the opinions of the people around her, including the staff and residents she identifies as her friends. She may feel that she is disappointing her friends with her inability to adapt to their standards of reality and possibility—particularly the standards they feel are realistic for her life.[32] RaRa cannot simply accept her disability and all the limitations that come with it, yet she may feel that acceptance is what her community expects of her. Guided by her shame, RaRa's hopes and dreams become secrets that she feels she needs to hide, yet in truth she does not want to keep her secrets to herself.

Since shame is behind her desire to name and submit her secrets, the act of naming and submitting her secrets becomes an antidote. The PostSecret project offers RaRa the best of both worlds: her secrets will remain anonymous, yet they will still become public. PostSecret is a perfect solution for RaRa's dilemma—except for the fact that her disability necessitates that she rely on another person to actually write down and submit her secrets. RaRa sees the chaplain and determines that she will be an acceptable scribe; perhaps she does not consider the fact that, in so doing, the chaplain will know her secrets. RaRa takes a risk by enlisting the chaplain's help. She cannot avoid revealing her deepest secrets to the chaplain, and she cannot be certain that the chaplain will not respond to her secrets by trying to squelch them. Thankfully, RaRa's risk pays off. The chaplain creates for RaRa an unchallenged space where RaRa can acknowledge and play with her secrets. Furthermore, the chaplain proves to be a trustworthy person who not only facilitates the play but also participates in it as a playmate and friend.

In subsequent conversations between RaRa and the chaplain, the two women consider ways in which the essence of RaRa's dreams might translate into reality, which involves considering real possibilities and naming the things that remain impossible. RaRa and the chaplain do not avoid considering the harsh realities of RaRa's life with a disability. These considerations are possible, though, because of this particular conversation, in which RaRa and the chaplain join together in an exercise of playful truth-telling. The chaplain has established their friendship as a safe, nonjudgmental space where all subjects are welcome and where all of RaRa's thoughts are treated with dignity and compassion. In her pastoral friendship with her chaplain, RaRa can share her deepest dreams for her life without being ashamed of them.[33]

RaRa's secrets are her hopes and dreams for her life. They speak to the most authentic part of her identity, which is often obscured by the unavoidable accommodations she must make for her disability. Were RaRa to permanently hide these secrets from the world, she might forget that her secrets exist—and forget who she really is.[34] RaRa is not "a disabled woman." She is a woman, living with a disability, who has hopes and dreams for her life that are just as valid as the hopes and dreams of women who are not living with disabilities like hers. Even so, at the time of this pastoral conversation, she seems to feel a sense of shame about her hopes and dreams as if she is not entitled to them. By keeping her hopes and dreams to herself as secrets, RaRa is withholding herself from others and compromising their ability to see and know her fully.

Theologically, RaRa's understandable withholding of herself from others compromises her capacity for mutual openness and therefore compromises her ability to live into the full co-humanity for which God created her. She cannot be fully seen by and known to others. Her fears and her shame prevent her from wanting to be open with others. Authentic co-humanity depends on people's willingness to be known to one another.[35] Openness, though, is risky in that it requires people to entrust themselves to others and move beyond their fears of being known. Openness involves people trusting that another person wants to know them and, likewise, wants to be known. In short, openness involves giving oneself over to a friendship in spite of the risks it poses. As RaRa's pastoral friend, the chaplain is not simply functioning as RaRa's scribe. She is also functioning as the facilitator of RaRa's co-humanity. In sharing her secrets with the chaplain, RaRa did just that. She takes the risk of being seen and known, secrets and all. What begins as the chaplain doing something for RaRa that any other staff member could do becomes a sacred moment of truth-telling, vulnerability, and, ultimately, trust.

RaRa needs some acknowledgment that her secrets are worth telling. She needs to know that she has the right to dream of a future with hope. As a minister in service to the God whose plans for all of God's children include a future with hope (Jeremiah 29:11), the chaplain can acknowledge the value of RaRa's secret hopes and dreams within the context of their pastoral friendship. By holding her secrets close, as the chaplain did, and by following through with RaRa's requests to write them down exactly as she stated them and mail them to Post-Secret, the chaplain not only validates RaRa's hopes and dreams but also helps ease some of RaRa's feelings of shame that emerge from her lack of self-esteem and threaten her ability to trust others. The chaplain's intentional decision to refrain from editing RaRa's longings but instead to copy them exactly as she states them conveys to RaRa a resounding sense of affirmation that her desires are good and do not need to be suppressed. By the power and presence of the Holy Spirit at work in their pastoral play, RaRa's truth-telling is transformed from an act of confession to a bold acknowledgment of the person God has created RaRa to be. RaRa's secrets become the means by which she is able to share and celebrate her authentic, God-given self with another and recognize that she is just as human—and just as beloved—as everyone else.

CONCLUSION: HAVE A SEAT

Bill, Jerry, and RaRa, each in their own way, invite their chaplain to sit beside them. They do not want her to sit at a distance and offer them words of wisdom. Instead, they want her to join them in connecting with their true selves—selves that they need the chaplain to acknowledge as good. Each conversation is different, yet each care receiver needs to be heard in a safe, unchallenged space. In each conversation, the chaplain intentionally works to foster a safe, creative space in which they can explore together the care receiver's needs in the manner that is most appropriate for that individual. This, after all, is the only way that the chaplain can truly sit and be present with each of these individuals in the ways that they most need her to be present. She could have easily "stood over" them by insisting that they talk to her on her terms.[36] In order for them to be able to trust her as a pastoral friend, they need to be able to share with her on their own terms and in their own words—or, as in Bill's case, in silence.

This chaplain understands her pastoral friendship with Bill, Jerry, and RaRa as existing within the larger framework of their friendship with God, which is possible because of Jesus Christ who is their mediator. Jesus reveals God's love to them and also makes known their love and gratitude to God.[37] Friendship with God is the essence of every human's calling. The same Christ who mediates this friendship with God also enables human friendships with one another, including pastoral friendships. Jesus Christ is the "hidden center" of all pastoral friendships and enables these friendships to flourish through the presence and power of the Holy Spirit[38] Christ is the "hidden center" of the chaplain's friendships with Bill, Jerry, and RaRa, even though they never acknowledge Christ's presence explicitly. Thus, while the chaplain is attentive to the psychological issues that are operative in their play and seeks to address them with the resources of psychology, she does so with an understanding that it is Christ who, through the Holy Spirit, is the ultimate source of any healing that occurs through their interactions.

Person-centered pastoral caregivers are called to have a seat beside people with disabilities—not above them or in front of them but beside them. As caregivers seek to offer care through collaborative pastoral friendships, they must be mindful of the risks that care receivers are taking when they agree to enter into this kind of collaboration. For example, RaRa wants to send her secrets into a nameless void, knowing that someone will read them with respect and without judgment. Yet in order to send her secrets anonymously, she has to reveal them to the chaplain. The irony of this situation is palpable and illustrates all too well the frustration that people with disabilities endure when they must rely on others for their every need. In this sense the initial ostensible need surrounding the chaplain's pastoral interaction with RaRa (her need to dictate her secrets) is simply an unfortunate by-product of RaRa's disability. In another sense, however, their pastoral interaction is a manifestation of their unavoidable, God-ordained co-humanity. It is unlikely that the reality of co-humanity will ever alleviate the frustration that RaRa and her fellow residents at the institution feel when their reliance on others is more a necessity than a choice. It does, however, illuminate the truth that God never intends anyone to be alone or to face their struggles alone. Humans have been created to share themselves with one another, helping one another with gladness as they seek to live faithfully into their particular callings. This is a central truth undergirding person-centered pastoral care. Pastoral care informed by this truth takes the form of a friendship, mediated by Christ through the power of the Holy Spirit, through which friends explore their challenges, needs, fears, and dreams, as well as strategies for moving forward in the vocations to which they have been called.

Person-centered pastoral caregivers are called to sit close beside those who seek to partner with them in a pastoral friendship. They are called to recognize that the Holy Spirit, poured out on *all* flesh, is sitting next to them, enabling their friendship despite the challenges that intellectual disability might otherwise bring. In a person-centered pastoral friendship centered in friendship with God, there can be healing—through coloring together, through creating a poem (and thereby affirming a sense of self), and even through risking giving voice to the hidden secrets of the heart. This is good news indeed.

SUGGESTIONS FOR FURTHER READING

Hunsinger, Deborah van Deusen. *Theology and Pastoral Counseling: A New Interdisciplinary Approach*. Grand Rapids: Eerdmans, 1995.

McNiff, Shaun. *Art Heals: How Creativity Cures the Soul*. Boston: Shambhala Publications, 2004.

Swinton, John. *Resurrecting the Person: Friendship and the Care of People with Mental Health Problems*. Nashville: Abingdon, 2000.

Vanier, Jean. *Encountering "the Other."* New York: Paulist, 2005.

5

Witnessing
Person-Centered Pastoral Care and the Church

By the power of the Holy Spirit that has been poured out on all flesh, the ministry of person-centered pastoral care can be shared among all of God's people. Bodies and minds shaped by disability are no less called to give care than they are to receive it, and the church does itself and the world a disservice if and when it overlooks this vital truth. The church needs to cultivate practices of care that involve all of God's people, regardless of ability or disability. The Apostle Paul identifies the church as the body of Christ, in which each part—including the weakest part—is vital to the functioning of the whole (1 Corinthians 12:12-26). However, if and when the Christian community forgets the body theology that shapes it, it risks alienating and stigmatizing people with disabilities through its attitudes and practices.[1] Faith communities have been known to ask people with disabilities and their families to look for other church homes because the people with disabilities cause too many disruptions in Sunday school or worship. Sadly, it is often easier for faith communities to turn away people and families than to seek out ways to welcome and embrace them. The Christian community's witness to all people—particularly to people with disabilities—must be a powerful witness of word and deed. The community and its members must, literally, embody the good news they have been called to share. They must speak Christ's words of welcome and friendship to all people and put those words into action, all the while knowing that it is Christ who, through the Holy Spirit, enables them to do both.[2]

Members of the body of Christ are kindred bodies and kindred minds—not by their own initiative, but by the gracious action of the God who, through Christ, has called them to fellowship with Him and with one another. They are kindred minds because God created them to be so. Regardless of ability or disability, Christians are called to a fellowship of kindred minds, sharing with each other the agape-love first shown by God in Christ. They are called to leap together with one another into friendship with God and to partner together to discover their particular vocations within that larger calling. In pastoral friendships, each friend can find strength for his or her life journey and, hopefully, clarity about ways to use his or her gifts in service to God. In and through pastoral friendships between people of all abilities and disabilities, the members of Christ's body bear witness to the world that God's loving and gracious calling has been extended to all bodies and all minds.

CHRISTIAN COMMUNITY, MINISTRY, AND THE CURE OF SOULS

A Ministry of Witness

People with intellectual disabilities both within and beyond faith communities need to hear the good news that God has equipped all of God's saints for ministry—including them. If a faith community fails to communicate God's love and grace to members with intellectual disabilities and ignores their particular, God-given gifts for ministry, then the community weakens its witness to the people with disabilities who are outside its doors. However, if the faith community embraces its members and prospective members with intellectual disabilities, embodies the gospel for them, and celebrates their unique gifts, then its outward witness to the world is strengthened.[3] When the church shares Christ's love boldly—in word and in deed—with its members with intellectual disabilities, the world can see something of Christ's love as well.[4]

Fundamentally, the Christian community is called to a ministry of prophetic witness—witness to its own members and witness to the world. The community is called to share and show God's radical love and grace in and through everything that it does and to do so in ways that are accessible for people of all abilities and disabilities. It is called to bear witness to the gospel of Christ by embracing people with intellectual disabilities as beloved children of God for whom Christ died and as fellow witnesses to God's saving work through Christ.[5] In everything that a faith community and its members do, the community proclaims the grace of God, made known in Christ, through whom all people have been reconciled to God and brought into covenant relationship with God.[6]

The Community's Witness in the Cure of Souls

Despite the Christian community's call to share God's great love with all people, the lack of welcome and friendship that people with intellectual disabilities often experience when seeking a church home may lead them to conclude that the good news of Jesus excludes them. Indeed, many people with disabilities sometimes feel that there is no place in the Christian community for them. The Christian community's witness, then, must communicate the gospel to people with even the most profound intellectual disabilities and genuinely welcome them to believe its good news and join in its mission, whether or not they have made—or even can make—an overt profession of faith.[7]

The community's ministry of witness finds expression in a variety of practices, including worship, preaching, Christian education, evangelism, mission efforts, fellowship, and prayer. The Christian witness also finds expression in its practices of pastoral care.[8] Person-centered pastoral care, as a component of the church's ministry of witness, is one of the many ways that people with intellectual disabilities can participate actively in the church's work in the world. Known also as the "cure of souls," pastoral care in general and person-centered pastoral care in particular address more than a person's psychological and spiritual issues. The object of the community's care is the whole person, which includes not only an embodied soul but also the promise and claim of God for every person—that is, every person's vocation.[9] The community's ministry of pastoral care not only attends to the needs of the whole person but also strengthens the person for the particular vocation to which God has called him or her.

While each person's vocation is unique, all people are called to participate in all facets of the community's ministry of witness. No

Christian is exempt from the responsibility of participating in the community's cure of souls. Even though some members of the community may seem to be more gifted than others in offering pastoral care, all members are called to care for one another.[10] While pastoral friendships certainly can and do exist between the pastor and members of the congregation, the pastor is not and should not be the congregation's sole caregiver. Since all members of Christ's body are called to participate in the church's ministry of care, pastoral friendships can and should exist among all members of the faith community. Pastoral care is a ministry in which all members of the community collaborate as both caregivers and care receivers. In so doing, the community and its members bear witness to the fundamental co-humanity that makes all people truly human. In caring relationships within the Christian community, brothers and sisters in Christ openly share their needs and concerns, listen actively and carefully to one another, and offer one another assistance.[11] In and through their mutual practices of care, brothers and sisters in Christ enact scripture's truth that each is a member of the other, and that both are equally valued members of the body of Christ (Ephesians 4:25; 1 Corinthians 12:12-26).

The same Holy Spirit that enables the co-humanity that makes all people fully human is also the source of care and cure in the community's ministry of pastoral care. Pastoral caregivers are not healers; they are agents of God's healing through the power of the Holy Spirit.[12] Since God is the source of healing, God can initiate healing at any time, in any place, in any way, and through any of God's children. Therefore, person-centered pastoral care, engaged in truly collaborative pastoral friendships, is one means by which God can foster healing.[13] Because of the creative work of the Holy Spirit within pastoral friendships, people with intellectual disabilities can be agents of God's healing for one another and for their typically functioning brothers and sisters in Christ. Pastoral caregivers living with intellectual disabilities can partner with friends of all abilities and disabilities, empowering them to move ever closer to living into their God-given vocations. Indeed, the Spirit-filled healing in the context of a person-centered pastoral friendship can enable both the caregiver and care receiver to recognize once again that they are necessary—indeed, invaluable—witnesses of Jesus Christ.[14]

Created to Care

Practices of mutual care and friendship in Christian community bear witness to the vital role that each community member plays in the church's ministry and reflect the handiwork of God who is Creator, Healer, Friend, and Author of vocation. Participation in the community's ministry of pastoral care involves the acts of giving and receiving, and people with intellectual disabilities are called to do both. Since all people have been created in the image of a fundamentally relational triune God, all people are meant to participate in caring relationships that accurately reflect the nature of God—relationships that are marked by respect, commitment, solidarity, and love.[15]

The creation narrative in Genesis muddies the waters of pastoral friendship and care when it describes the *imago Dei* as having dominion over creation. "Dominion" often connotes domination and, at its worst, an abuse of power in which the value of one life is depreciated by that of another.[16] However, when "dominion" of creation is understood more in terms of responsibility and stewardship, then it is clear that all human beings, created in the image of God, have been given the responsibility of caring for God's creation—not dominating it. To be faithfully and authentically human is to care for one another in relationships that reflect the very nature of a caring relational God.[17] All people are called to a life of giving and receiving care, not only as members of Christ's body but also as human beings created in the image of a God who is love and care. When people offer care to one another and receive care from one another, they demonstrate the fullness of their God-given humanity.

Since caregiving is a component of God-given humanity, the care that humans offer to one another is not a product of human ingenuity. Instead, the care that transpires between people is God's care, which has been entrusted to God's people and in which God's people have been invited to participate. People's care for one another is responsible care. In the ministry of care, Christians take responsibility for one another such that they empower one another to flourish and to be the people God has created then to be.[18] In other words, in their mutual ministry of care, Christians can work to enable one another to live into the particular vocations for which God has created them and to which God has called them. People with intellectual disabilities are called to participate in the life of the community as both responsible caregivers and gracious care receivers. People with more profound intellectual disabilities may offer responsible tangible care in the form of a strong quiet presence with brothers and sisters who are in need.[19] People whose disabilities are less profound may take a more active role in practices of caring, including praying for fellow members of the community, visiting those who are sick, and even seeking out ways to meet the needs of brothers and sisters in crisis.[20] Regardless of the shape of the care, people with intellectual disabilities need opportunities to both give care to and receive care from their fellow brothers and sisters in Christ. People with intellectual disabilities have been created to care, and the strength of the church's witness depends upon their full participation in its caring ministry.

CARING *WITH* PEOPLE WITH INTELLECTUAL DISABILITIES

Beyond "Us" and "Them"

By its very nature, the cure of souls is pastoral care with those who are in need; it is not a one-sided service in which one person simply offers care to another without any reciprocity. In the ministry of pastoral care, people move together through life's complexities, all for the sake of both individual and shared vocation. People with intellectual disabilities have been given their own gifts and capabilities as caregivers, but their potential is easily overlooked when typically functioning fellow Christians assume that people with intellectual disabilities are always only in need of care. Assumptions such as these, while inaccurate, often accompany the best of intentions, and with good reason. People with intellectual and developmental disabilities may, and often do, have more complex needs than others, and faith communities are the places where those needs can be met with competence, compassion, and enthusiasm.[21] However, by underestimating the caring capacities of their brothers and sisters with intellectual disabilities, typically functioning Christians risk focusing so much on caring for people with intellectual disabilities that they are unable to be present with them in pastoral friendships that might foster healing for all.[22] Indeed, the practice of being truly present with brothers and sisters in Christ is a carefully nuanced kind of hospitality. "Being with" is not simply a matter of "us" (those without noticeable disabilities) welcoming "them" (those with noticeable disabilities) into "our" community and serving "them." Instead, "being with" means that everyone is welcomed and included as they are, as unique individuals with unique gifts and needs, and are recognized as vital members of the body of Christ who can share in a common ministry and witness.

Hospitality in Christian community involves people with and without intellectual disabilities sharing their lives with one another, as opposed to one person offering a service to another.[23] For followers of Christ, this is as it should be. At God's table—in Christ's church—all people are guests of a gracious Host who is no respecter of persons. No one guest is more important or more powerful than another—each guest has a place of honor at this table.[24] The power dynamics so common in secular interactions between people with and without disabilities are trumped in Christian community by the politics and hospitality of Jesus. Authentic Christlike hospitality requires that all people move from their current positions of power or powerlessness to a shared position of mutuality and friendship.[25] While some people may need to relinquish power according to the world's standards, all people gain strength through friendships with one another that bear witness to Christ. Since God has welcomed and honored all people as guests and friends, all are free to welcome one another as friends, regardless of ability or disability. When typically functioning Christians embrace their brothers and sisters with intellectual disabilities with the hospitality of Christian friendship, they become partners in ministry and care. Embracing people with intellectual disabilities as true brothers and sisters in Christ enables them to do what they need and want to do: be caregivers as well and participate in the church's ministry of care to which they have been called.[26] When they are given the opportunity to share their gifts and graces with the community, both they and the community become stronger.[27]

Caring with Friends

Members of the body of Christ, who all have been formed in the image of a fundamentally relational God, are called to bear witness to

God's love for all of God's children by caring for one another through practices of mutual openness, listening, and assisting that are carried out in a spirit of gladness. The Christian community is a community of friends whose care for one another reflects the loving God who first befriended each of its members.[28] Because the friendships among fellow brothers and sisters in Christ are to reflect God's friendship with God's children, Christian friendships are both shaped and shepherded by God's agape-love. God alone enables the kind of mutual love and care that takes place in Christian friendship, because God has first loved each friend.[29] Christian love is not a product of human intellect or will. In fact, there is nothing human about it. God alone, through the power of the Holy Spirit, equips and empowers all people to love. Not even the most profound intellectual disability can keep a person from participating in a loving, caring, pastoral friendship.[30] To paraphrase the Apostle Paul, God and God's love are the forces at work in every person that enable him or her to do God's work as a good and faithful friend (Philippians 2:13).

Guided by the mysterious work of the Holy Spirit, the pastoral friendship between fellow members of the body of Christ is a sacred space. In the sacred space of a pastoral friendship, friends with and without intellectual disabilities can love one another with God's love and participate in God's friendship—the friendship to which all people have been called. Pastoral friendship is also the space within which Christians can work together to discern the shape of their particular vocations within their shared calling to be God's witnesses.[31] Even though vocational discernment can be a product of pastoral friendships, no one should seek out a pastoral friendship as a means to this end, nor should a typically functioning person befriend someone with intellectual disabilities simply to help him or her discover a vocation. While friends are certainly partners in discernment and ministry, Christians should not seek out pastoral friendships with one another simply because they perceive each other—or even themselves—as useful. To be sure, friends—including friends with intellectual disabilities—can and do make important contributions to each other's lives and can lend clarity to each other's vocational identities. After all, these contributions are part of the giftedness of friendship. Even so, typically functioning Christians must guard against implying—even inadvertently—that the vocation of people with intellectual disabilities is to facilitate their own self-discovery.[32]

In life together as the body of Christ, pastoral friendships with people with intellectual disabilities are to be as mutually loving, supportive, and life-giving as pastoral friendships with anyone else. Approaching any pastoral friendship with utilitarian motives compromises the *koinonia* that is the true end of authentic Christian friendship, as well as the church's ministry of pastoral care. *Koinonia* refers to the fellowship among Christians that is grounded in the life of God; when Christians join together in fellowship, they also join in fellowship with the triune God.[33] Since the goal of Christian vocation is friendship with God, and since God's love and friendship fund Christians' friendships with one another, it comes as no surprise that the telos of human friendship is koinonia: the loving friendship between God and God's children.[34] In other words, the telos of Christian friendship with people with intellectual disabilities (and those without) lies in the friendship itself, which is mediated by Jesus Christ and lived out in a spirit of gladness through practices of mutual sharing, listening, and assistance.

THE DISTINCTIVENESS OF PERSON-CENTERED PASTORAL CARE IN THE CHURCH

Since koinonia is the telos of both friendship and pastoral care within the body of Christ, a person-centered approach to pastoral care is a natural fit within the church's caring ministry. Like the secular approaches to person-centered support that inform it, person-centered pastoral care involves deep listening to the needs and dreams of a care receiver, as well as collaboration with the care receiver in identifying his or her gifts and finding ways to use them within the community. As an activity of Christian friendship and a ministry of Christ's church, person-centered pastoral care has unique characteristics that distinguish it from its secular counterparts. When, in a pastoral friendship, Christians engage one another gladly in the practices of mutual sharing, listening, and assisting, they do not do so as means to an end. Rather, these practices are ends in themselves, as they fund the koinonia that is central to Christian care. In this collaboration and through the power of the Holy Spirit, Christians with and without intellectual disabilities can experience their true humanity, understood in terms of friendship with God and with one another.

In person-centered pastoral friendships, communion with one another and with God is the central aim. This does not mean that partners in a pastoral friendship must avoid or abandon the kinds of conversations and processes that are engaged in secular person-centered support. It does mean, however, that secular processes and conversations are not the reason for the pastoral friendship, nor are they the goal of it.[35] As people share with and listen to one another in pastoral friendship, they will undoubtedly reveal their needs, dreams, hopes, and fears. After all, these are aspects of their humanity. Were they to withhold these thoughts from one another, they would threaten the authenticity of their humanity and, indeed, their friendship. Likewise, if people deny one another the opportunity to offer assistance as they address aspects of themselves, they rob one another of the opportunity to participate in a mutually caring relationship. Clarity of identity and vocation is likely to emerge from the "play" of a person-centered pastoral friendship. Yet these points of clarity are outgrowths of the friendship, not the friendship's raison d'être. Recall the pastoral friendships between the chaplain and Bill, Jerry, and RaRa. For each of these three individuals, their friendship with the chaplain was, in itself, a source of care and a conduit of God's healing. The clarity they achieved regarding the specific issues they addressed was simply an outgrowth of the friendship they shared.

Just as it is God who calls God's children together into pastoral friendships, it is God who is the author of the healing that may occur within friendship's sacred space.[36] The pastoral friendship itself is a conduit for God's transforming work in the lives of each friend. In a person-centered pastoral friendship, the lines between caregiver and care receiver are necessarily and wonderfully blurred. In some encounters, one person may function more as a caregiver, while the other person receives care in relation to specific needs or issues that he or she has shared. In other encounters, their roles will be reversed. In pastoral friendships, each participant is both a giver and a receiver as guided by the Spirit's work and shaped by God's love and care. In the context of the church's caring ministry, person-centered pastoral friendships demonstrate to the world that people of all abilities and disabilities can share the transforming love and care of the God who has called all people to lives of discipleship.[37]

CULTIVATING PERSON-CENTERED PASTORAL CARE IN THE MINISTRY OF THE CHURCH

Faith communities can strengthen their witness to all people by cultivating practices of person-centered pastoral care in which people of all abilities and disabilities can minister to one another. Person-centered pastoral care is not one-size-fits-all; the shape of person-centered pastoral care will vary from one congregation to another and from one friendship to another. Just as there are a variety of gifts among the membership of the body of Christ, there can be different kinds of pastoral friendships within congregations, each of which will reflect the particularities of the friends it comprises. The particularities of size and content will differ from one friendship to another according to the needs, gifts, and personalities of the friends involved. Person-centered planning is an art, and so, too, are person-centered pastoral friendships. Regardless of its particular shape, each is a partnership guided and nourished by God's Holy Spirit that bears witness to God's love.

First Things First: Creating a Space for Friendship

While pastoral friendship is the safe, hospitable space within which friends can share with one another their needs and dreams and discern the Spirit's presence in their midst, the Christian community is the context—the space—within which these friendships thrive. Just as it takes time, energy, and courage to nurture any faithful friendship, it takes time, energy, and courage for a congregation to become a space in which pastoral friendships can flourish—particularly friendships that include people with intellectual disabilities.[38] Faith communities can begin to create an ethos of welcome and friendship by making sure their meeting spaces and facilities are accessible for people with disabilities. The presence of elevators, ramps, and recreational areas suitable for children of all abilities and disabilities can convey to people with disabilities and their families a congregation's spirit of welcome and its desire to cultivate friendships with people living with disabilities.[39]

Once people with disabilities have been welcomed into a faith community's physical space, the community can extend their welcome by being willing to communicate the gospel in a variety of ways. Sometimes, people with intellectual disabilities need to have enhanced or alternative communication techniques available so that they can understand the gospel in worship, in religious education, and in fellowship activities. Alternative communication techniques can include amplification of sound in worship; sermons or services available on CD; sign language; worship components presented through music, drama, or other visual aids; and Sunday school curricula that are accessible to children and adults operating at a variety of cognitive levels.[40]

Perhaps the most challenging barrier that people with intellectual disabilities face in seeking inclusion in a faith community is the attitude of community members. Members of faith communities are sometimes uncomfortable around people with developmental and intellectual disabilities because they do not know how to interact or communicate with people who may interact and communicate differently than their typically functioning counterparts. As a result, people with disabilities may either be ignored or isolated by faith communities, or they are treated as objects of pity. Ideally, faith communities could regard people with disabilities first as children of God with gifts and graces to share and only second as people who have disabilities.[41] People with disabilities need to be able to sense a congregation's hospitality from the moment they arrive in its gathering space, not simply because the building is accessible (though this is extremely important). A faith community and its members must communicate that they not only welcome people with disabilities but also desire them to join as participants in their common life.[42] Arriving at this level of hospitality is no small task, and it takes time. Nurturing an ethos of welcome and inclusion is an ongoing journey for faith communities that may begin with an assessment of their current level of hospitality, followed by intentional prayer and discernment about the steps they need to take to make all people feel welcome. Next, congregations can establish a team of members from all areas of congregational life who can examine and develop strategies for improving the congregation's attitudes, policies, and practices regarding people with disabilities. Through intentional prayer and concrete action, a faith community can become a body of believers that reflects the deep love and radical hospitality of the God who calls all people to friendship with God and one another.[43]

Beyond the Welcome: Cultivating Pastoral Friendships

Faith communities must stay attuned to the physical, psychological, and spiritual needs of all their members—including members with disabilities—and do all that they can to meet these needs.[44] At the same time, faith communities must recognize the often-subtle difference between addressing needs and including people.[45] People with intellectual disabilities need and want to be included in the life and work of the community as equal participants—and contributors.[46] The challenge for faith communities is to move beyond initial practices of hospitality to practices that nurture mutual, person-centered pastoral friendships as the context of the congregation's ministry of pastoral care. The community's transition to deeper practices of care and friendship does not mean that the practical problem-solving efforts on behalf of people with disabilities need to be abandoned. Rather, the community's efforts to meet needs and solve problems are best engaged within the context of mutually caring and supportive friendships.

In order to engage in authentic, person-centered pastoral friendships with people with and without intellectual disabilities within faith communities, all members must be willing and able to recognize each other as partners in caring; each member is both guest and host, care receiver and caregiver. This kind of mutual recognition is born from the community's strong commitment to nurture mutuality in its members' relationships with one another. Each member needs to recognize that every fellow member's presence in his or her life is, in itself, a gift. To be sure, each individual member has gifts that need to be acknowledged and engaged for the strengthening of the community. Even so, the focus of relationships should not be a person's gifts but rather the person as gift.[47] Part of recognizing each community member as gift is being open to the possibility of receiving hope, wisdom, and guidance from members who are typically only identified as care receivers. Openness to receiving care from others requires the awareness that each member of the community has the capacity to make a difference in another life and in the life of the community.[48]

Like any authentic friendship, a pastoral friendship involves "kindred minds" coming together because of shared interests or beliefs. One important component of person-centered thinking and planning is "capacity thinking": attention to a person's gifts, strengths, and interests as opposed to his or her deficiencies, shortcomings, and disabilities. Disability is not a barrier to friendship when the person with the disability is recognized as a gift whose strengths and interests will enhance the life and witness of the community. Pastoral friendships can take many different forms. A pastoral friendship may consist of a person with a disability and another member of the congregation coming together as "faith partners" in a relationship of mutuality and care.[49] Faith partners may choose to sit together in worship services and assist each other in reading scripture or singing hymns. They may seek ways to lead the congregation in worship or contribute to the congregation's mission endeavors. And they may also help each other consider how they might use their God-given gifts and interests in ways that enrich their own lives and glorify God.[50]

Pastoral friendships can be shared by two people or by a group of three or more. A pastoral friendship group can be a safe space within which each friend is not only welcomed but encouraged to name and explore their issues, needs, and dreams, all the while receiving care and support from the other friends in the group. United in Christ and guided by the Holy Spirit, the members of a pastoral friendship group can invest in one another's lives through mutual listening, sharing, and helping, and sustain one another through their shared testimony to God's faithfulness.[51] Ideally, a pastoral friendship group in a faith community would include people with and without intellectual disabilities, each of whom contributes to the life and work of the group as a whole—including each member extending care to his or her fellow members in whatever ways he or she can. Group members may need to exercise creativity and improvisation to ensure that members with intellectual disabilities are included and capable of full participation.

A pastoral friendship group flourishes when there is clarity among its members regarding the purpose around which the group is formed, the nature of group membership (including its duration and whether and when new members will be able to join), and its commitment to confidentiality.[52] Adding to the strength of a group are the structure of its meetings and open, honest attention to group process. A group may choose to begin its meeting with welcoming, centering, and silence, followed by reading and reflecting on a passage of scripture. The group may want to explore creative ways of engaging scripture during this time, particularly for members with intellectual disabilities who may receive scripture best through pictorial or other sensory representations.

After a time of quiet corporate reflection and prayer, the group could enter a time in which each member shares from his or her own process of discerning the shape of God's calling in his or her life and communicating his or her needs to the group. This would be an appropriate time for the group to consider ways that each group member might take responsibility for addressing some of the needs of the person seeking assistance. For example, if one group member is concerned about procuring transportation between her group home and church, another group member could volunteer to coordinate transportation each week. A group member struggling to pay bills correctly and on time might seek assistance from someone in the group who could assist him in this task. Attention to the practical details and needs of people's lives is one way of helping them to live into the particular vocation to which they believe God is calling them. People with intellectual disabilities who feel called to live independently or hold a particular job may be sustained in their efforts with the help and support of their brothers and sisters in Christ who will, at some point, seek and receive their help as well.

During this time of sharing, group members might also share words of encouragement and edification with one another, noting times that they have seen Christ working in each other's lives.[53] For example, members might share with each other how the care they have received from fellow members has informed their lives of faith. Members may acknowledge losses, traumas, or grief they have suffered and share what they need in order to experience healing.

They may name the gifts they see in other members of the group and acknowledge the gifts that others see in each of them.[54] By considering and answering these kinds of questions within the context of a pastoral friendship group, people with intellectual disabilities have the opportunity to make a tangible contribution not only to the group process but also to the lives of individual members as they acknowledge what they see in others and how others have shaped their lives. Furthermore, rich opportunities for healing, growth, and enriched community involvement emerge when people with disabilities hear their gifts and graces acknowledged by fellow brothers and sisters in Christ.

After a time of sharing, the group might participate in a time of silent and spoken prayer in which each member is invited to follow the Spirit's leading in interceding on one another's behalf. Again, this is a time when the group can use its creativity and imagination to foster a rich time of prayer for the group as a whole and especially for people with intellectual disabilities. For example, if the Holy Spirit guides the process of a particular meeting toward thoughts and feelings that evoke lament, the group might decide to structure its time of prayer as a time for group members to write and share their own lament psalms (with one or more members offering assistance, as needed, to members with intellectual disabilities) in addition to offering prayers of intercession for one another.[55]

As the group prepares to conclude their time together, members might choose to recite the Lord's Prayer or sing a song together. These concluding moments offer the group another opportunity to engage creative worship practices. Perhaps the group would want to say the Lord's Prayer using elementary signs, gestures, and movements for each part of the prayer.[56] The interactive Lord's Prayer and other creative approaches to worship are likely accessible to people functioning at a variety of cognitive levels and, thus, foster participation among all group members. After concluding its structured time together, pastoral friendship groups would benefit from reflecting on and assessing the group process.[57] By engaging in reflection on the group process as part of the life of the group, each member of the group demonstrates its commitment to making sure that all its members—especially those with intellectual disabilities—are fully included and, therefore, fully capable of giving and receiving pastoral care with their friends.

There are a variety of gifts but the same Spirit. Likewise, there are a variety of ways in which members of faith communities can cultivate pastoral friendships within which the variously gifted members of Christ's body may share their gifts of care with one another. Intellectual disability is not a barrier to koinonia. When members of faith communities recognize people with intellectual disabilities as gifted, caring friends, they discover that without the presence and contributions of all of God's people the church is incomplete.

CONCLUSION

On the first Sunday of each month, a Baptist congregation in a small town in southwest Virginia celebrates the Lord's Supper, in which they both remember the sacrifice of Christ's body and blood and embrace their own identity as the body of Christ in the world. Once the bread and juice have been consumed and the final hymn has been sung, all members of the congregation join hands and sing four lines of a well-known hymn as a blessing for their week:

> Blest be the tie that binds
> Our hearts in Christian love;
> The fellowship of kindred minds
> Is like to that above.[58]

For many years the fifth pew from the front was occupied, every Sunday, by three or four residents from a group home located approximately three blocks from the church. Each of these individuals had an intellectual disability. They were active congregants: they participated in Sunday school, worship, and other special events; they welcomed church members into their home for parties and other get-togethers; and they joined the rest of the congregation in celebrating births and grieving deaths. And, on the first Sunday of every month, they too joined hands with those around them and acknowledged that "the fellowship of kindred minds is like to that above." They were truly a part of that congregation.

One of the group home residents and regular worship attendees was a gentleman named Mickey. Mickey was the object of much observation and curiosity for a little girl in the congregation, who watched him regularly during Sunday worship services. She could not understand why Mickey swayed back and forth during the hymns while everyone else politely stood still and stared at their hymnals. She certainly did not doubt the legitimacy of his actions, nor did she think that because of his intellectual disability he was somehow closer to God than everyone else in the room, perhaps. While the little girl

always appreciated Mickey, she never considered the possibility that
they could be friends, caring for, learning from, and encouraging each
other as friends do. The little girl knew that Mickey and his friends
were part of her faith community, but they seemed too different for her
to ever imagine them as her friends. Many years later, that grown-up
little girl would realize how essential Mickey really was to her childhood life of faith. Church simply was not church for her without him.

Mickey and that little girl could have been friends. After all, they
were part of the same "fellowship of kindred minds" that had been
created and called together by the God who, through Christ and by
the power of the Holy Spirit, enables and enlivens every friendship.
The fellowship of kindred minds that is the body of Christ is a fellowship of people of all abilities and disabilities, who are all are vital
to the health of the body. Indeed, every mind is precious; every mind
is "kindred" to every other mind. And indeed, the fellowship of kindred minds is, by design, "like to that above." God created God's people to be a community of caring friends. God has created and called
God's people to be friends who share joy and sorrow, gladly giving
and receiving the gift of one another. Through Christ who, by the
power of the Holy Spirit, mediates human friendships with God and
with one another, all people can find healing in and through pastoral friendships—healing that enables them to live into the particular
vocations that God has given them.

With Christ mediating friendships with God and with one
another, intellectual disability does not pose a threat to mutuality
within friendships. What does threaten mutuality, however, is fear
and uncertainty about the possibility of engaging in authentic friendships with individuals who typically functioning Christians could
never imagine relating to as "kindred minds." Person-centered pastoral care is not easy. Pastoral friendships are not easy, regardless of abilities or disabilities. In the process of cultivating pastoral friendships,
challenges will emerge, probably more quickly than the bonds of love,
compassion, and understanding will be forged. Even so, the calling
for all Christians to care for one another as holy friends is a calling
that all Christians need to accept together, trusting that the God who
calls God's people will also sustain them as they seek to enrich their
common life.

Pastoral friendship is a calling that Christians accept together. It is a Christian practice—an activity in which Christians participate together as a grateful response to God's presence in their lives and in the world.[59] People with intellectual disabilities can and should be welcomed as participants in the church's ministry and, in particular, in its practices of caring. As the context for the church's practices of caring, pastoral friendship challenges to the all-too-common assumption that people with intellectual disabilities can only be recipients of the church's ministry and not partners in it. Mediated by Christ through the power of the Holy Spirit, person-centered pastoral friendships are spaces in which people with and without intellectual disabilities share their needs, issues, and dreams as a practice of care. In pastoral friendships, all of God's children can be strengthened to live into the particular vocations to which they have been called, regardless of ability or disability. By cultivating collaborative, person-centered practices of care in the context of pastoral friendships, the church can strengthen its witness as a place of belonging for people with intellectual disabilities. The God who created all people has given all people dreams to dream and vocations to embrace, none of which are disabled by disability. The church needs dreamers of all abilities to carry its witness to the world. By God's grace, may it always endeavor to welcome the dreamers with gladness and call them friends.

SUGGESTIONS FOR FURTHER READING

Carter, Erik W. *Including People with Disabilities in Faith Communities: A Guide for Service Providers, Families, and Congregations.* Baltimore: Paul H. Brookes Publishing, 2007.

Conner, Benjamin T. *Amplifying Our Witness: Giving Voice to Adolescents with Developmental Disabilities.* Grand Rapids: Eerdmans, 2012.

Hunsinger, Deborah van Deusen. *Pray without Ceasing: Revitalizing Pastoral Care.* Grand Rapids: Eerdmans, 2006.

Swinton, John. *From Bedlam to Shalom: Towards a Practical Theology of Human Nature, Interpersonal Relationships, and Mental Health Care.* New York: Peter Lang, 2000.

Yong, Amos. *The Bible, Disability, and the Church: A New Vision for the People of God.* Grand Rapids: Eerdmans, 2011.

Notes

INTRODUCTION

1   Francis Collins, director of the National Center for Human Genome Research in the United States, advocates for the proliferation of genetic research, saying, "The most unethical approach of all would be to insist that genetic research be stopped; because if it were, those individuals, present and future, who suffer from the ravages of genetic diseases would be doomed to hopelessness." See Francis Collins, foreword to *Playing God? Genetic Determinism and Human Freedom*, by Ted Peters (New York: Routledge, 1997). See also Hans Reinders, *The Future of the Disabled in Liberal Society: An Ethical Analysis* (South Bend, Ind.: University of Notre Dame Press, 2000), 1. According to theologian Gerald McKenny, genetic experts' "unquestioned commitments to technological control of the body for the sake of eliminating 'misery and necessity'" constitutes what he calls "the Baconian Project." See Gerald P. McKenny, *To Relieve the Human Condition: Bioethics, Technology, and the Body* (Albany: State University of New York Press, 1997). The National Council of Churches addresses the dangers of this perspective on both disability and biotechnology in its policy statement on biotechnology. The statement reads: "The use of tools and processes declared to be neutral and value free, and designed to relieve suffering, holds great promise when they can support the lives of people with disabilities or alleviate unnecessary pain or suffering. But biotechnology becomes profoundly disquieting to many with disabilities when disabling conditions or predictions are equated with life long suffering, imperfection, or disease. When those personal and social values are combined with the power of technology to prevent the birth of a child with a disability or defect, the possibility of a new eugenics fueled by social values, market forces, and personal choice, rather than official policy, becomes quite real." See National Council of Churches, USA, "Fearfully and Wonderfully Made: A Policy on Human Biotechnologies Adopted November 2006," accessed February 7, 2012.

2   Reinders, *Future of the Disabled*, 2.
3   John Swinton, "Introduction: Reimagining Genetics and Disability," in *Theology, Disability and the New Genetics: Why Science Needs the Church*, ed. John Swinton and Brian Brock (New York: T&T Clark, 2007), 2–4; cf. Reinders, *Future of the Disabled*, 40.
4   Swinton, "Introduction," 4.
5   Amy Laura Hall, *Conceiving Parenthood: American Protestantism and the Spirit of Reproduction* (Grand Rapids: Eerdmans, 2008), 285.
6   Mary B. Mahowald, "Aren't We All Eugenicists Anyway?" in Swinton and Brock, *Theology, Disability and the New Genetics*, 105. During my second pregnancy (at age thirty-six), my obstetrician instructed his office staff to make an appointment for me with a genetic counselor without even asking me if I wanted to undergo genetic testing. After pushing the doctor to explain the need for testing, he finally admitted that it would not be necessary if I already knew that I did not want to terminate the pregnancy.
7   Mahowald, "Aren't We All Eugenicists," 99. In his introduction to this edited volume, John Swinton echoes Mary Mahowald's essay by distinguishing between the kind of eugenics that are implicit in prenatal testing and that which occurred during the Nazi holocaust—and the distinction is worth mentioning here. Few, if any, of the ethicists and theologians who make connections between eugenics and current uses of genetic technology would equate these practices with the atrocities perpetrated by the Nazis. While those practices were state-sanctioned and often coerced, present-day pregnancy terminations are a matter of choice within their legal parameters. See Swinton, "Introduction," 4.
8   Thomas Reynolds, *Vulnerable Communion: A Theology of Disability and Hospitality* (Grand Rapids: Brazos, 2008), 33. Reynolds suggests that the culture has subscribed to a "cult of normalcy," such that "an image is cast onto those whose lives disrupt the status quo, manifesting a lack or deficiency of what is construed as standard, ordinary, and familiar."
9   Reinders, *Future of the Disabled*, 52. John Swinton addresses this inaccurate presumption as well, noting that much of the suffering that people with Down syndrome endure has more to do with the way they are devalued by society and less to do with the genetic, physical, or cognitive components of their disorder. See Swinton, "Introduction," 5. At the same time, as Thomas Reynolds reminds us, we cannot overlook the fact that people with disabilities often do experience bodily impairments, and "they are nonetheless bodily affected by those impairments, making possible the experience of disability." See Reynolds, *Vulnerable Communion*, 26.
10   Benjamin T. Conner, *Amplifying Our Witness: Giving Voice to Adolescents with Developmental Disabilities* (Grand Rapids: Eerdmans, 2012), 5–6.

CHAPTER 1

1   Ann Ulanov and Barry Ulanov, *The Healing Imagination: The Meeting of Psyche and Soul* (Mahwah, N.J.: Paulist, 1991), 9–10.

2   According to the American Association on Intellectual and Developmental Disabilities (AAIDD), *disability* "refers to personal limitations that are of substantial disadvantage to the individual when attempting to function in society." See the AAIDD's 2008 document "Frequently Asked Questions on Intellectual Disabilities and the AAIDD Definition," accessed March 2, 2017. An *intellectual* disability is "a disability characterized by significant limitations both in intellectual functioning and in adaptive behavior, which covers a range of everyday social and practical skills." See the AAIDD Web page "Frequently Asked Questions on Intellectual Disability," accessed March 2, 2017.

3   Ulanov and Ulanov, *Healing Imagination*, 5–6.

4   David Race, ed., *Leadership and Change in Human Services: Selected Readings from Wolf Wolfensberger* (London: Routledge, 2003), 3. The term "mental retardation" and its derivatives were commonplace in the mid- to late twentieth century and were, therefore, the terms that advocates for people with disabilities used in their writings. Within the last fifteen years, the terms "mental retardation" and "mentally retarded" have begun to be replaced, with greater frequency, by the term "intellectual disability." In fact, the President's Committee on Mental Retardation was recently renamed the President's Committee for People with Intellectual Disabilities. See President's Committee for People with Intellectual Disabilities, "Fact Sheet," accessed April 22, 2015. In 2007 the American Association on Mental Retardation (AAMR) changed its name to the American Association on Intellectual and Developmental Disabilities (AAIDD). The terms are synonymous, yet "intellectual disability" is considered less offensive to individuals with disabilities. It reflects a commitment to work toward a greater understanding of "disability identity" and to strengthen support for people with intellectual disabilities in order to facilitate their flourishing. See the AAIDD's "Frequently Asked Questions on Intellectual Disability."

5   Wolf Wolfensberger, excerpt from "The Bad Things That Typically Get Done to Devalued People," in Race, *Leadership and Change*, 33–34. Jean Vanier discusses the loneliness that comes with the wound of life-wasting. He says, "[Loneliness] can be a source of apathy and depression, and even of a desire to die. . . . It is the loneliness we find in those who fall into depression, who have lost the sense of meaning in their lives, who are asking the question born of despair: What is left? I once visited a psychiatric hospital that was a kind of warehouse of human misery. Hundreds of children with severe disabilities were lying neglected, on their cots. There was a deadly silence. Not one of them was crying. When they realize that nobody cares, that nobody will answer them, children no longer cry. It takes too much energy. We cry out only when there is hope that someone may hear us." See Jean Vanier, *Becoming Human* (New York: Paulist, 1998), 8–9.

6   Robert Kugel, "Why Innovative Action?" in *Changing Patterns in Residential Services for the Mentally Retarded*, ed. Robert Kugel and Wolf Wolfensberger (Washington, D.C.: President's Committee on Mental Retardation, U.S. Printing Office, 1969), 8.

7   Bengt Nirje, "The Normalization Principle and Its Human Management Implications," in Kugel and Wolfensberger, *Changing Patterns*, 181–88.

8   Wolf Wolfensberger, *Normalization: The Principle of Normalization in Human Services* (Toronto: National Institute on Mental Retardation, 1972), 28.

9   Wolfensberger, "Bad Things," 76–83.

10 Race, *Leadership and Change*, 5. Wolfensberger helped develop this innovative program.

11 John O'Brien and Connie Lyle O'Brien, "The Origins of Person-Centered Planning: A Community of Practice Perspective," in *Implementing Person-Centered Planning: Voices of Experience*, ed. John O'Brien and Connie Lyle O'Brien (Toronto: Inclusion Press, 2002), 35.

12 O'Brien and O'Brien, "Origins of Person-Centered Planning," 38–39. Other PASS participants asked similar questions, including "What are the likely consequences for the people we met if current practice does not change?" and "What is this person at greatest risk for, if we do not change his or her life?"

13 O'Brien and O'Brien, "Origins of Person-Centered Planning," 29.

14 John O'Brien and Beth Mount, *Make a Difference: A Guidebook for Person-Centered Direct Support* (Toronto: Inclusion Press, 2005), 38. According to O'Brien and Mount, "impairment" refers to "an individual difference that results in a need for access, accommodation or assistance if the person is to function effectively in settings that matter to the person." "Deficiency," then, might be understood as an insufficiency or absence of qualities, characteristics, and skills necessary to participate fully in a given society according to the norms of that society (36).

15 O'Brien and Mount, *Make a Difference*, 42.

16 Beth Mount, "The Art and Soul of Person-Centered Planning," in O'Brien and O'Brien, *Implementing Person-Centered Planning*, 145.

17 Karl Barth, *Church Dogmatics*, vol. 4, pt. 3.2, *The Doctrine of Reconciliation* (London: T&T Clark, 2004), 482. Elsewhere, Barth makes a clear and careful distinction between calling in terms of vocation and calling in terms of what he calls "the divine summons." The latter consists of God's summons to a person to claim his or her special freedom to live in obedience to the will and word of God. Vocation consists of the particularity of the individual and the life circumstances in which God has created and situated him or her. God claims this particularity and uses it in God's summons to obedience. See Karl Barth, *Church Dogmatics*, vol. 3, pt. 4, *The Doctrine of Creation* (London: T&T Clark, 2004), 598.

18 Barth, *Church Dogmatics*, vol. 3, pt. 4, 620–23. Socioeconomic status and family and community roles constitute what Barth calls the "external limitations" of vocation. The "internal limitation" of vocation includes a person's "specific endowment and inclination as these are related to his psycho-physical structure and disposition and as they result in his particular receptive and productive ability, fitness and usefulness."

19 Barth, *Church Dogmatics*, vol. 3, pt. 4, 620–23. Jürgen Moltmann emphasizes this idea as well, saying, "God takes people at the point where he reaches them and

just as they are. He always accepts people quite specifically, as man or woman, Jew or Gentile, old our young, black or white, disabled or not disabled, and so forth, and puts their lives at the service of the coming kingdom which renew the world. So if we ask about the charismata of the Holy Spirit we mustn't look for the things we don't have. We have to discern who we are, and what we are, and how we are, at the point where we feel the touch of God on our lives." See Jürgen Moltmann, *The Source of Life: The Holy Spirit and the Theology of Life* (Minneapolis: Fortress, 1997), 56.

20 Barth, *Church Dogmatics*, vol. 4, pt. 3.2, 575.

21 Barth, *Church Dogmatics*, vol. 3, pt. 4, 627.

22 Barth, *Church Dogmatics*, vol. 3, pt. 4, 599. Barth distinguishes between vocation "in the usual sense" (a job) and vocation "in a comprehensive sense" (the sum of all aspects of a person's life that may or may not include employment).

23 "WHO Definition of Health," preamble to the constitution of the World Health Organization as adopted by the International Health Conference, New York, June 19–22, 1946. Signed June 22, 1946, by the representatives of sixty-one states (official records of the World Health Organization, no. 2, p. 100) and entered into force April 7, 1948.

24 Bioethicist Daniel Callahan addresses the inadequacy of the WHO's definition of health. He says, "One can be healthy without being in a state of 'complete physical, mental, and social well-being.' That conclusion can be justified in two ways: (a) because some degree of disease and infirmity is perfectly compatible with mental and social well-being; and (b) because it is doubtful that there ever was, or ever could be, more than a transient state of 'complete physical, mental, and social well-being,' for individuals or societies; that's just not the way life is or could be. . . . The demands which the word 'complete' entails set the state for the worst false consciousness of all: the demand that life deliver perfection." See Daniel Callahan, "The WHO Definition of 'Health,'" *Hastings Center Studies* 1, no. 3 (1973): 77–87, reprinted in *On Moral Medicine: Theological Perspectives in Medical Ethics*, ed. Stephen E. Lammers and Allen Verhey, 2nd ed. (Grand Rapids: Eerdmans, 1998), 253–61.

25 Barth, *Church Dogmatics*, vol. 3, pt. 4, 356–58. More specifically, Barth identifies health as "the strength to be as man."

26 Morris Maddocks, *The Christian Healing Ministry* (London: SPCK, 1990), 10–11. Maddocks notes that in the Old Testament, the scope of shalom extends beyond the personal. Shalom is well-being among individuals, communities, and even nations. Likewise, health involves more than just individual well-being. As Joel Shuman and Keith Meador explain, "We are not truly human as long as we are not at home with ourselves, at peace with our neighbors, and living harmoniously with that part of the earth we call home." See Joel James Shuman and Keith G. Meador, *Heal Thyself: Spirituality, Medicine, and the Distortion of Christianity* (New York: Oxford University Press, 2003), 12.

27 Robert E. Korth, "Your Special Friends: Misconceptions, Temptations, and Surprises in Ministry with Adults Having Mental Retardation," in *Reaching Out to*

Special People: A Resource for Ministry with Persons Who Have Disabilities, ed. Jim Pierson and Robert Korth (Cincinnati: Standard Publishing, 1989), 19–30.

28 Robert Fife and Jim Pierson, "A Model of Compassion: The Role of the Church for Persons Having Disabilities," in Pierson and Korth, *Reaching Out to Special People*, 135.

29 Jim Pierson, "Introduction: Close Enough to Notice," in Pierson and Korth, *Reaching Out to Special People*, 14.

30 Dean Preheim-Bartel et al., *Supportive Care in the Congregation: Providing a Congregational Network of Care for Persons with Significant Disabilities*, rev. ed. (Goshen, Ind.: Mennonite Publishing Network, 2011), 19–20.

31 Bill Gaventa compares the supportive care group to the circle of support that is a foundational component of person-centered planning. He says, "The circle of support model draws upon the willingness of others to do something specific once they have had a part in hearing and defining the needs. It also helps them realize they are a part of a support circle, that it is not all up to them. They have a valued part that makes a difference, but it is not solely their responsibility." See William C. Gaventa, "Creating and Energizing Caring Communities," in *Caregiving and Loss: Family Needs, Professional Responses*, ed. Kenneth J. Doka and Joyce Davidson (Washington, D.C.: Hospice Foundation of America, 2003), 72. A circle of support collaborates with the supported person to come up with concrete strategies for providing support; it is not an interdisciplinary team that comes up with a plan and presents it to the family and the person with a disability. Instead, "It is a process that assumes that the more heads and hearts you have the more creative people can be, that people may be more willing to take on specific pieces of a plan they have figured out together rather than shying away from taking on the whole thing" (70).

32 Gaventa, "Creating and Energizing," 48.

33 Preheim-Bartel et al., *Supportive Care in the Congregation*, 50–54, 57–58.

34 Preheim-Bartel et al., *Supportive Care in the Congregation*, 45–46, 55.

35 Preheim-Bartel et al., *Supportive Care in the Congregation*, 77.

36 Jennie Weiss Block, *Copious Hosting: A Theology of Access for People with Disabilities* (New York: Continuum, 2002), 159.

37 Brett Webb-Mitchell, *Beyond Accessibility: Toward Full Inclusion of People with Disabilities in Faith Communities* (New York: Church Publishing International, 2010), 114. Webb-Mitchell, for example, uses the idea of "co-creation" to describe the shared ministry of people with and without disabilities within the body of Christ. In this shared ministry, people "of differing abilities and limitations" worship, teach, and learn "in an atmosphere of acceptance."

38 Webb-Mitchell, *Beyond Accessibility*, 127.

39 Conner, *Amplifying Our Witness*, 5.

40 Conner, *Amplifying Our Witness*, 5–6.

41 Deborah van Deusen Hunsinger, *Theology and Pastoral Counseling: A New Interdisciplinary Approach* (Grand Rapids: Eerdmans, 1995), 12. As Hunsinger explains, Karl Barth is a helpful *pastoral* theological dialogue partner because

of the ways in which his theological approach informs the church's ministry of pastoral care and our reflections on the nature of that care. Barth intends his theology to be a theology of the church. As such, Barth situates the ministry of pastoral care squarely within the mission and work of the church. At the same time, however, Barth is not averse to considering and adopting insights from other fields—including the social sciences—in the church's ministry, thus making his theology an asset for interdisciplinary thinking and dialogue. In his discussion of the "cure of souls," Barth says of the community as a caregiver, "To be serviceable to [a care receiver] in this respect, to show him the way to it, is the unique beginning of what the community can do for him in the cure of souls. Seldom or never will this occur without the unconscious—and why not the conscious?— presupposition and sometimes application of various forms of general or secular and therefore neutral psychology, psychogogics, and psychotherapy." See Barth, *Church Dogmatics*, vol. 4, pt. 3.2, 886.

42 James Loder, *The Logic of the Spirit: Human Development in Theological Perspective* (San Francisco: Jossey-Bass, 1998), 32. Loder recalls T. F. Torrance's claim that trying to understand creation apart from God's revelation in Jesus Christ is akin to "pre-Einsteinian understandings of geometry in relation to physics."

43 Hunsinger, *Theology and Pastoral Counseling*, 64–66. Barth uses the Chalcedonian pattern to guide his discussions on a variety of topics, including his understanding of the relationship between the human soul and body (Church Dogmatics, vol. 3, pt. 2, The Doctrine of Creation [London: T&T Clark, 2004]), and the relationship between healing and forgiveness (Church Dogmatics, vol. 1, pt. 2, The Doctrine of the Word of God, [Edinburgh, T&T Clark, 1956], 189). Hunsinger herself adapted the pattern for use in interpreting theological and psychological material in pastoral counseling.

44 Hunsinger, *Theology and Pastoral Counseling*, 65.

45 Hunsinger, *Theology and Pastoral Counseling*, 75. Hunsinger draws on Barth's usage of a Chalcedonian pattern of thought to demonstrate the ways in which it can function as the theoretical context and framework for the ministry of pastoral counseling.

46 Deborah van Deusen Hunsinger, "An Interdisciplinary Map for Christian Counselors: Theology and Psychology in Pastoral Counseling," in *Care for the Soul*, ed. Mark McMinn and Timothy Phillips (Downers Grove, Ill.: InterVarsity, 2001), 226–27.

47 Hunsinger, *Theology and Pastoral Counseling*, 226.

48 Jack Pearpoint and Marsha Forest, "The Ethics of MAPS and PATH," in *A Little Book about Person-Centered Planning*, ed. John O'Brien and Connie Lyle O'Brien (Toronto: Inclusion Press, 1998), 95.

49 Barth, *Church Dogmatics*, vol. 3, pt. 4, 632–33.

50 Barth, *Church Dogmatics*, vol. 3, pt. 4, 629.

CHAPTER 2

1 Pearpoint and Forest, "Ethics of MAPS and PATH," 94.

2   D. W. Winnicott, "The Theory of the Parent-Infant Relationship," in *The Mat-urational Processes and the Facilitating Environment* (Madison: International Universities Press, 1965), 43.

3   D. W. Winnicott, "Ego Integration in Child Development," in *Maturational Processes*, 57.

4   D. W. Winnicott, *Playing and Reality* (London: Routledge, 2006), 15–16.

5   Winnicott, "Parent-Infant Relationship," 37.

6   Art therapist Shaun McNiff believes that the therapist's functioning as a caretaker of safe, creative space is fundamental to the therapeutic process and essential to an individual's processes of healing and self-discovery. He says, "As a keeper of the [therapeutic] studio, my function is to maintain the creative and healing energy of the environment. I do this through example, support, and constant guidance." McNiff also contends that the major distinction between therapy in an art studio and therapy in a clinical setting is found in a studio therapist's willingness to let go of control "so that things outside our current awareness can come forward." See Shaun McNiff, *Art Heals: How Creativity Cures the Soul* (Boston: Shambhala Publications, 2004), 24–28.

7   D. W. Winnicott, "Ego Distortion in Terms of True and False Self," in *Maturational Processes*, 145.

8   D. W. Winnicott, *Human Nature* (New York: Schocken Books, 1988), 104.

9   Peter Leidy, "Whose Life Is It Anyway?" in O'Brien and Mount, *Make a Difference*, 102.

10 Art psychotherapist Cindy Caprio-Orsini comments on the all-too-frequently narrow and unimaginative approaches to supporting trauma victims with disabilities. She writes, "Even in an era of 'progressive mental health treatment' there are an astounding number of people who believe that those with limited intellectual capacities, minimal verbal communication, or a disability are not able to benefit from trauma therapy. Better and easier to keep them medicated or preoccupied with simple tasks (tasks that even a rat could perform). . . . Medication and menial tasks do not take away the core problem." Caprio-Orsini's words are true not only with regard to the particular kind of care given to trauma victims with disabilities, but also to care that people with intellectual and developmental disabilities in general so often receive. See Cindy Caprio-Orsini, *A Thousand Words: Healing Through Art for People with Developmental Disabilities* (Quebec: Diverse City Press, 1996), v.

11 Winnicott, "Ego Distortion," 146.

12 Winnicott, "Ego Distortion," 146.

13 Winnicott, "Ego Distortion," 147.

14 Leidy, "Whose Life Is It Anyway?" 103.

15 Leidy, "Whose Life Is It Anyway?" 102.

16 Winnicott, *Playing and Reality*, 64.

17 Winnicott, *Playing and Reality*, 3.

18 Winnicott, *Playing and Reality*, 3.

19 Winnicott, *Playing and Reality*, 130.

20 Winnicott, *Playing and Reality*, 76–86.

21 Winnicott, *Playing and Reality*, 69.

22 Winnicott, *Playing and Reality*, 75.

23 Winnicott, *Playing and Reality*, 75–76. Dorothy Martyn's psychoanalytic work with children illustrates the benefits of collaborative play in the therapeutic setting. When she begins her play therapy with a child, she spends a good bit of time simply mirroring back "the child's own being." This mirroring allows the child to be seen, which may be a new experience for him or her. In this mirroring process, Martyn follows the children's lead and, in so doing, encourages the cultivation of their true selves. See Dorothy Martyn, *The Man in the Yellow Hat: Theology and Psychoanalysis in Child Therapy* (Atlanta: Scholars Press, 1992), 103–4.

24 Winnicott, *Playing and Reality*, 73. Winnicott does not limit the notion of creativity to the creation of particular works of art. His notion of creative living is much more holistic. He says, "It is true that a creation can be a picture or a house or a garden or a costume or a hairstyle or a symphony or a sculpture; anything from a meal cooked at home. It would perhaps be better to say that these things could be creations. The creativity that concerns me here is a universal. It belongs to being alive" (91).

25 Winnicott, *Playing and Reality*, 87. Winnicott says, "Contrasted with [creative living] is a relationship to external reality which is one of compliance, the world and its details being recognized but only as something to be fitted in with or demanding adaptation. Compliance carries with it a sense of futility for the individual and is associated with the idea that nothing matters and that life is not worth living. In a tantalizing way many individuals have experienced just enough of creative living to recognize that for most of their time they are living uncreatively, as if caught up in the creativity of someone else, or of a machine."

26 Winnicott, *Playing and Reality*, 91.

27 Winnicott, *Playing and Reality*, 91. Winnicott makes the troubling suggestion that the aliveness that comes with creativity "must be less strikingly significant in terms of animals or of human beings with low intellectual capacity than it is with human beings who have near average, or high intellectual capacity."

28 Winnicott, *Playing and Reality*, 91.

29 McNiff, *Art Heals*, 5.

30 Winnicott, *Playing and Reality*, 74.

31 Winnicott, *Playing and Reality*, 75.

32 Mary Falvey et al., *All My Life's a Circle: Using the Tools—Circles, MAPS and PATHS* (Toronto: Inclusion Press, 1997), 17–28.

33 O'Brien and Mount, *Make a Difference*, 13–14.

34 O'Brien and Mount, *Make a Difference*, 11.

35 Judith Snow, "The Power in Vulnerability," in O'Brien and O'Brien, *Little Book about Person-Centered Planning*, 12. The late Judith Snow was a disability rights advocate. She was also a person with disabilities who relied on the care of direct support workers.

36 Snow, "Power in Vulnerability," 13.

37   O'Brien and Mount, *Make a Difference*, 92.

38   Mount, "Art and Soul of Person-Centered Planning," 147.

39   Pearpoint and Forest, "Ethics of MAPS and PATH," 95.

40   Ann Belford Ulanov and Alvin Dueck, *The Living God and Our Living Psyche: What Christians Can Learn from Carl Jung* (Grand Rapids: Eerdmans, 2008), 70. Ulanov contends that this imaginative space is not at all a threat to faith but is, instead, faith's servant.

41   Winnicott, *Playing and Reality*, 19.

42   Ann Belford Ulanov, *Finding Space: God, Winnicott, and Psychic Reality* (Louisville, Ky.: Westminster John Knox, 2001), 22–23. In *The Birth of the Living God*, Ana-Maria Rizzuto explores the origin, cultivation, and role of individuals' God-representations. She suggests that in these conceptions of God, God functions psychologically as a special kind of transitional object "created from representational materials whose sources are the representations of primary objects." One part of a God-representation derives from what a child "finds" in his primary object relationships, while the other part derives from what the child is able to "create" as a means of fulfilling his needs. This "pet God" (as Rizzuto calls it) informs the child's—and later, adult's—self-image: "Consciously, preconsciously, or unconsciously, God, our own creation, like a piece of art, a painting, a melody . . . will, in reflecting what we have done, affect our sense of ourselves." See Ana-Maria Rizzuto, *The Birth of the Living God: A Psychoanalytic Study* (Chicago: University of Chicago Press, 1979), 178–79.

43   Ulanov, *Finding Space*, 23–24.

44   Ulanov and Dueck, *Living God*, 77.

45   In this context, Ann Ulanov suggests that "image" constitutes the variety of ways that we come to understand God: "some of us visually, others of us through body sensations, textures, smells, sounds." See Ulanov and Dueck, *Living God*, 70.

46   Ulanov, *Finding Space*, 26.

47   Ulanov, *Finding Space*, 30.

48   Ulanov, *Finding Space*, 33–34. Ulanov writes, "Whatever we run from will turn up in our subjective-object God-images. . . . Our pet gods bring forward our missing pieces."

49   Ulanov, *Finding Space*, 31.

50   Ulanov and Dueck, *Living God*, 74–75. Jung calls this the "transcendent function" of the human psyche.

51   Ulanov and Dueck, *Living God*, 75–76.

52   Ulanov, *Finding Space*, 36.

CHAPTER 3

1   Christopher de Vinck, *The Power of the Powerless* (New York: Doubleday, 1988), 10–11.

2   Many of the letters de Vinck received in response to his account of life with Oliver express appreciation for de Vinck's powerful testimony to the value and potential inherent in every human life (de Vinck, *Power of the Powerless*, 31–38).

De Vinck gives the credit to Oliver, who demonstrated "the power of the powerless" (31).

3   De Vinck, *Power of the Powerless*, 9.

4   Barth, *Church Dogmatics*, vol. 3, pt. 4, 607. Barth makes a distinction between "vocation" (*Beruf*)—this "special place of responsibility"—and a more general notion of "calling" or "divine summons" (*Berufung*). As Kuzmič explains, "For Barth, there is one divine calling [*Berufung*] which is differentiated in relation to each person's vocation (*Beruf*) as well as the individual's *charisma* and *diakonia*." See Rhys Kuzmič, "*Beruf* and *Berufung* in Karl Barth's *Church Dogmatics*: Toward a Subversive Klesiology," *International Journal of Systematic Theology* 7, no. 3 (2005): 268. The English translation of *Church Dogmatics* uses the word "vocation" for both *Beruf* and *Berufung*, which, as Kuzmič demonstrates, invites misconceptions and misunderstandings about Barth's foci in vol. 3, pt. 4, and vol. 4, pt. 3.2. For the sake of clarity, I will use the term "calling" as I consider Barth's discussion of *Berufung* in vol. 4, pt. 3.2, and its relevance to the work of person-centered pastoral care.

5   This is not to suggest divine determinism, however. Barth rejects the idea that human beings are simply "passive instruments used by God, possessing no relevant agency of their own." Human agency is an important aspect of Barth's thought, but he does not wish to emphasize it "at the expense of divine grace." God's work through the Spirit enables our action, yet we remain the actors. As Barth says, "It is not the work of the Holy Spirit to take from us our own proper capacity as human beings, or to make our capacity simply a function of his own overpowering control. Where he is present, there is no servitude but freedom" (*Church Dogmatics*, vol. 4, pt. 2, The Doctrine of Reconciliation [London: T&T Clark, 2004], 785). The work of the Holy Spirit frees us for action. Likewise, the Holy Spirit frees people with intellectual disabilities for action in ways that can only be attributed to the miracle of grace. See George Hunsinger, "The Mediator of Communion," in *Disruptive Grace: Studies in the Theology of Karl Barth* (Grand Rapids: Eerdmans, 2000), 163.

6   Daniel Price, *Karl Barth's Anthropology in Light of Modern Thought* (Grand Rapids: Eerdmans, 2002), 128.

7   Barth, *Church Dogmatics*, vol. 4, pt. 3.2, 491.

8   Joseph Tomilio III, "Called by Grace: Elucidating and Appropriating the Doctrine of Vocation in Karl Barth's Church Dogmatics," *The New Mercersburg Review* 34 (2004): 5. Tomilio acknowledges the frequent misinterpretation of vocation as a human endeavor. He elucidates Barth's contention that vocation (calling), as described in vol. 4, pt. 3.2, is not only the third pillar of salvation (along with justification and sanctification) but also an act of grace by God through Jesus Christ.

9   Hans Reinders, *Receiving the Gift of Friendship: Profound Disability, Theological Anthropology, and Ethics* (Grand Rapids, Eerdmans, 2008), 301–2.

10 Barth, *Church Dogmatics*, vol. 4, pt. 3.2, 490–91. "To be sure, the assertion [that all people 'stand in the light of life'] must not cut across or in any sense compete

with the further statement that 'I cannot by my own reason or strength believe in
Jesus Christ my Lord, or come to Him, but the Holy Ghost has called me by the
Gospel.' Our assertion concerns the foreordination and predisposition of every
man for the supremely particular event of his vocation to be a Christian. If with
the necessary humour and good will there may be recognized in it the element
of truth in Tertullian's *anima humana naturaliter christiana*, there is obviously no
reference to any immanent human capacity to be a Christian, nor to any fruit of
the human work of Christian activity generally perceptible in the world, nor to
any such ideal results, but to the eminently real determination of all humanity
by the supreme reality of the divine act of salvation for and to it and the living
divine Word within it."

11 Barth, *Church Dogmatics*, vol. 4, pt. 3.2, 519. Barth says, "It is not in view of what
we Christians . . . have experienced, let alone felt as our vocation, but in view
of the One who has honoured us with His vocation, that we venture, and must
venture, to speak of this process with the distinction which we have accorded it."

12 Barth, *Church Dogmatics*, vol. 4, pt. 3.2, 508–9.

13 Barth, *Church Dogmatics*, vol. 4, pt. 3.2, 512.

14 Barth, *Church Dogmatics*, vol. 4, pt. 3.2, 515–16.

15 In 1 Corinthians 1:25-27 the Apostle Paul writes, "God's foolishness is wiser than
human wisdom, and God's weakness is stronger than human strength. Consider
your own call, brothers and sisters: not many of you were wise by human standards, not many were powerful, not many were of noble birth. But God chose
what is foolish in the world to shame the wise; God chose what is weak in the
world to shame the strong" (NRSV).

16 Henri Nouwen suggests as much in his commentary on Oliver de Vinck's life.
Nouwen says, "[It] breaks with all human logic, all intelligent predictions, all
normal norms of success and satisfaction. It turns everything upside down. It
speaks not only about the power of the powerless, but also about love offered
by those who cannot speak words of love, joy created by those who suffer griev-
ously, hope given by those whose lives are complete failures, courage enkindled
by those who cannot make the slightest move on their own. In a world that so
much wants to control life and decides what is good, healthy, important, valuable and worthwhile, [it] makes the shocking observation that what is hidden
from 'the learned and the clever' is revealed 'to mere children' (Matt. 11:25)."
See Henri Nouwen, introduction to *The Power of the Powerless*, by Christopher
de Vinck (New York: Doubleday, 1988), xvii.

17 Barth, *Church Dogmatics*, vol. 4, pt. 3.2, 510.

18 Barth, *Church Dogmatics*, vol. 4, pt. 3.2, 521.

19 Karl Barth, *Church Dogmatics*, vol. 2, pt. 1, *The Doctrine of God* (Edinburgh:
T&T Clark, 1957), 274. George Hunsinger elaborates on how the triune nature
of God informs the telos of God's call. He says, "Seeking and creating fellowship
are definitive of God's reality. As in eternity so also in time God is essentially a
God of sociality, the triune deity who loves in freedom. . . . It is in fellowship that
God wills to be our God and wills us to be God's people." See George Hunsinger,

How to Read Karl Barth: The Shape of His Theology (New York: Oxford University Press, 1991), 173.

20 Barth, *Church Dogmatics*, vol. 4, pt. 3.2, 536.

21 We must be careful to acknowledge, however, the intimacy, integrity, and asymmetry that characterize the relationship between Jesus and the Christian. The mutual self-giving between the two renders them a "single totality." At the same time, each maintains an individual identity: "In their fellowship both become and are genuinely what they are, not confounding or exchanging their functions and roles nor losing their totally dissimilar persons." Finally, we must remember that Christ and the Christian each occupy a different conceptual status: "[Jesus] is unique as the One who in His life and death was humiliated and exalted in the place and for the sake of all, as the One in whom the reconciliation of the world to God and the justification and sanctification of all were accomplished. In all this He has no assistant nor fellow-worker to accompany Him, let alone any *corredemptor* or *corredemptrix*." Quotations from Barth, *Church Dogmatics*, vol. 4, pt. 3.2, 539–41. See also Hunsinger, *How to Read Karl Barth*, 174–79.

22 Barth, *Church Dogmatics*, vol. 4, pt. 3.2, 512.

23 Barth, *Church Dogmatics*, vol. 4, pt. 3.2, 544–45.

24 Barth, *Church Dogmatics*, vol. 4, pt. 3.2, 530.

25 Barth, *Church Dogmatics*, vol. 4, pt. 3.2, 544.

26 This is Hans Reinders' primary concern in *Receiving the Gift of Friendship*. Reinders actually critiques Barth's theological anthropology because he believes it inadvertently presumes that human agency is operative.

27 Brett Webb-Mitchell recounts such a line of reasoning implicit in one well-meaning pastor's sermon. He says, "In one church, after a chorus of people with mental retardation sang the anthem for Sunday morning worship, the pastor began talking about angels. He started by talking about the angels in the Bible. . . . Then he compared the sometimes sweet, frequently off-key sound of the present chorus of people with mental retardation as being a contemporary 'sound of angels.' But by labeling them as angels, he inadvertently robbed them of the richness of being human and left them with the barrenness of one-dimensional, postcard innocence." See Brett Webb-Mitchell, *Dancing with Disabilities: Opening the Church to All God's Children* (Cleveland: United Church Press, 1996), 48.

28 Robert Perske, "An Attempt to Find an Adequate Theological View of Mental Retardation," in *The Pastoral Voice of Robert Perske*, ed. William C. Gaventa and David L. Coulter (New York: Haworth Press, 2003), 43–44.

29 For example, Craig Modahl recounts his experience with his friend Kevin, who has lived with Modahl's family for more than twenty years. Kevin's intellectual disability prevents him from speaking and communicating beyond a few adaptive signs for basic needs. When Modahl, his wife, and Kevin went to their Catholic church to receive the Eucharist, their priest told them that "by the larger church requirements, he was not permitted to give Kevin the 'host'—the bread, the body of Christ. Kevin did not respond properly when the host was presented

nor had he ever expressed a clear statement of faith." Modahl goes on to recount that "at one point, it was mentioned to us that if we could get Kevin to respond verbally with 'amen' or some similar affirmation, he would likely be permitted to participate." Craig Modahl, "Finding a Place at the Table," *Journal of Religion, Disability and Health* 13, nos. 3–4 (2009): 320–22.

30 Hans Vium Mikkelsen, *Reconciling Humanity: Karl Barth in Dialogue* (Grand Rapids: Eerdmans, 2010), 97n14. Barth's perspective resembles the philosophy most notably promoted by German philosopher Martin Buber. Inspired by Jewish mysticism, Buber developed his philosophy of dialogue in his acclaimed work *Ich und Du*, which was first published in 1923 and translated into English as I and Thou by Ronald Gregor Smith fourteen years later (New York: Charles Scribner's Sons, 1937). Mikkelsen offers a helpful discussion of Barth's and Buber's respective conceptions of the I-Thou relationship and argues that Barth underestimated the influence of Buber's work on his own anthropology.

31 Karl Barth, *Church Dogmatics*, vol. 3, pt. 2, *The Doctrine of Creation* (London: T&T Clark, 2004), 218. "To be sure, God is One in Himself. But He is not alone. There is in Him a co-existence, coinherence and reciprocity. God in Himself is not just simple, but in the simplicity of His essence He is three-fold—the Father, the Son and the Holy Ghost. He posits himself, is posited by Himself, and confirms Himself in both respects, as his own origin and also as his own Goal. He is in himself the One who loves eternally, the One who is eternally loved, and eternal love; and in this triunity he is the original and source of every I and Thou, of the I which is eternally from and to the Thou and therefore supremely I."

32 Mikkelsen, *Reconciling Humanity*, 97, 106.

33 Mikkelsen, *Reconciling Humanity*, 97, 106.

34 Barth, *Church Dogmatics*, vol. 3, pt. 2, 221. Barth writes, "He who is already glorified by the Father in His relationship to Him is again glorified in them, in His relationship to men. Thus the divine original creates for itself a copy in the creaturely world. There could be no plainer reference to the *analogia relationis* and therefore the *imago Dei* in the most central, i.e., the Christological sense of the term."

35 Barth, *Church Dogmatics*, vol. 3, pt. 2, 274.

36 Reinders, *Receiving the Gift of Friendship*, 238.

37 Barth, *Church Dogmatics*, vol. 3, pt. 2, 245–48.

38 Mikkelsen, *Reconciling Humanity*, 109. Barth says, "One thing at least is certain. A pure, absolute and self-sufficient I is an illusion, for as an I, even as I think and express this I, I am not alone or self-sufficient, but am distinguished from and connected with a Thou in which I find a being like my own, so that there is no place for an interpretation of the 'I am' which means isolation and necessarily consists in a description of the sovereign self-positing of an empty subject by eruptions of its pure, absolute and self-sufficient abyss." See Barth, *Church Dogmatics*, vol. 3, pt. 2, 245–46.

39 Amos Yong uses the term "reimagining" to describe his own project in *Theology and Down Syndrome: Reimagining Disability in Late Modernity* (Waco, Tex.: Baylor University Press, 2007). In this project, Yong employs what he calls the

"pneumatological imagination" which, he says, is "an epistemic posture shaped in part by the biblical narratives of the Holy Spirit and in part by the Christian experience of the Spirit" (11). Drawing on the account of Pentecost found in Acts 2, Yong contends that "the many tongues of Pentecost signify both the universality of the gospel message and its capacity to be witnessed to by those who derive from the many nations, cultures, ethnicities, and languages of the world." Based on this contention, Yong identifies the threefold significance of a pneumatological imagination. First, it allows us to consider "the perennial metaphysical and philosophical question concerning the one and its relationship to the many" using a framework that is explicitly theological. Second, the pneumatological imagination "provides a theological rationale for preserving the integrity of differences and otherness, but not at the expense of engagement and understanding." Last, it encourages Christians to listen to a variety of discourses through which, as through the many tongues of Pentecost, the Holy Spirit might speak (11–12). By engaging a pneumatological imagination, an interpretation of Barth's theological anthropology can be broadened in ways that are at once faithful to Barth's thought and attentive to the particularities of intellectual disability that are not explicitly addressed in Barth's text.

40   Barth says that when humans are willing to see and be seen, "We give each other an insight into our being. And as we do this, I am not for myself, but for thee, and Thou, for me, so that we have a share and interest in one another. This two-sided openness is the first element of humanity. Where it lacks, and to the extent that it lacks, humanity does not occur. To the extent that we withhold and conceal ourselves and therefore do not move or move any more out of ourselves to know others and to let ourselves be known by them, our existence is inhuman, even though in all other respects we exist at the highest level of humanity." See Barth, *Church Dogmatics*, vol. 3, pt. 2, 251.

41   Barth, *Church Dogmatics*, vol. 3, pt. 2, 253.

42   Barth, *Church Dogmatics*, vol. 3, pt. 2, 253.

43   Barth, *Church Dogmatics*, vol. 3, pt. 2, 254–55.

44   Price, *Karl Barth's Anthropology*, 149.

45   Price, *Karl Barth's Anthropology*, 150. Barth writes, "If I and Thou really see each other and speak with one another and listen to one another, inevitably they mutually summon each other to action." See Barth, *Church Dogmatics*, vol. 3, pt. 2, 260–61. Barth is also careful to note that while authentic, mutually giving relationships involve people offering each other help and care, there is no room for altruism. One person cannot take upon himself or herself the concerns and responsibilities of another.

46   Barth, *Church Dogmatics*, vol. 3, pt. 2, 265–66.

47   Barth, *Church Dogmatics*, vol. 3, pt. 2, 265.

48   Mikkelsen, *Reconciling Humanity*, 117–18.

49   Disability theologian Hans Reinders, while generally lauding Barth's Trinitarian relational concept of the *imago Dei*, argues that Barth's theological anthropology cannot be universally human. He says, "Even though Barth believed this

human freedom [to be in relationship] to be grounded in the humanity of Christ, in the sense of being constituted by a relationship, this view is not incompatible with the view he intended to leave behind [the view that the image of God is somehow intrinsic in human beings]. It is perfectly possible to account for the primordial concept of relationship in terms of the Hegelian principle of reflection that begins with the subject as the 'in itself' freely positing the objective 'for itself' in order to overcome the separation in the 'in and for itself.' According to this principle, the 'I' reaches out toward the other in order to find itself enriched in the process. In contemporary theological anthropology, 'relationality' is in fact often understood as a necessary condition for becoming precisely this kind of enriched being. While such an account may certainly result in a richer and less individualistic concept of being human, it does not abandon but rather presupposes the concept of the human being as individual rational substance." See Reinders, *Receiving the Gift of Friendship*, 243.

50 Reinders, *Receiving the Gift of Friendship*, 244.

51 Barth, *Church Dogmatics*, vol. 3, pt. 2, 350.

52 Barth, *Church Dogmatics*, vol. 3, pt. 2, 349–50. As Daniel Price notes, Barth's conception of the relationship between body and soul reflects his desire to move beyond the dualistic view of personhood that has dominated Western thought for almost fifteen hundred years. This view posits a self-sufficient soul that is "encumbered" by a body. Barth is arguing that "soul and body are dynamically related" and cannot exist apart from one another (Price, *Karl Barth's Anthropology*, 248). Amos Yong draws on the theory of emergence to make a related claim as a means of proposing a theological anthropology that is inclusive of people with intellectual disabilities. This theory, borne out of dialogue between experts in the field of cognitive neuroscience, contends that human consciousness is dependent on physical properties of the brain but cannot be reduced to or completely explained by them (Yong, *Theology and Down Syndrome*, 170–71). Yong proposes an emergentist view of the soul in which the soul is constitutive of but irreducible to "the sum of the body's biological parts," including mental faculties (170).

53 Barth, *Church Dogmatics*, vol. 3, pt. 2, 349, 418. Barth says, "As [man] is grounded, constituted, and maintained by God as soul of his body, and thus receives and has the Spirit, there occurs the rule of the soul and the service of the body. And in this occurrence man is a rational being" (419). His appeal to rationality is somewhat troubling from a disability perspective. However, Barth acknowledges that the term "rational being" is ambiguous and needs to be understood in a "true and comprehensive and not restricted sense" (419). Since it is the mysterious work of the Spirit who empowers and enables the soul and body, and not any faculty intrinsic to the human being, we need not limit our understanding of "rational being" to people who appear to have reason and will.

54 Barth, *Church Dogmatics*, vol. 3, pt. 2, 355–56.

55 Daniel Price rightly notes that Barth's concept of the basic form of humanity is not a reference to Christian love (agape). Price says, "[Barth] is talking about the

human being as a human being, not necessarily filled with the Holy Spirit, but simply fulfilling his or her human nature" (*Karl Barth's Anthropology*, 154). The I-Thou relationship should not be equated with (or limited to) the Christian community, in which relationships are marked by God's gracious love through the power of the Holy Spirit. However, if human beings are what they are because of God's work through the Spirit—if, as Barth says, the Spirit is "the basis of soul and body," then it stands to reason that the Spirit is involved in the living of every human life, Christian or not. Amos Yong says as much: "Not only does the breath of God give life to *ha adam*, it also informs our consciousness (traditionally understood in terms of the human conscience), our interpersonal and intersubjective relationship with others (traditionally understood in terms of the Holy Spirit as the communion of Christian fellowship; 2 Cor 13:13), and our relationship with God (traditionally understood in terms of the Spirit's drawing us into fellowship with God). In all of these ways, I suggest that the Holy Spirit is at work in all human lives to shape us in the image of God in Christ" (Yong, *Theology and Down Syndrome*, 190–91).

56   As Amos Yong poignantly explains, "People with and without disabilities can be caught up in the Spirit's blowing across the world, and in the process, their lives converge even as what emerges are new lives enriched one by the other." See Yong, *Theology and Down Syndrome*, 186.

57   Karl Barth, *Church Dogmatics*, vol. 4, pt. 2, 745. Barth insists that his anthropology is not a discussion of Christian love but rather a description of the basic form of humanity regardless of one's faith commitments (or lack thereof). Here, though, Barth is saying that the fullness of one's humanity is realized in Christian love, made possible through the Holy Spirit.

58   Barth, *Church Dogmatics*, vol. 4, pt. 2, 745.

59   Barth, *Church Dogmatics*, vol. 4, pt. 2, 747.

60   Yong, *Theology and Down Syndrome*, 187.

61   Barth claims that no human being has an innate capacity for knowledge of or faith in God. He says, "Faith is not one of the various capacities of man, whether native or acquired. Capacity for the Word of God is not among these. The possibility of faith as it is given to man in the reality of faith can be understood only as one that is loaned to man by God, and loaned exclusively for use." See Karl Barth, *Church Dogmatics*, vol. 1, pt. 1, *The Doctrine of the Word of God* (Edinburgh: T&T Clark, 1975), 238.

62   Tracy Demmons, "Being in Encounter: Toward a Post-critical Theology of the Knowledge of God for Persons with Intellectual Disabilities: With Special Reference to Karl Barth's *Church Dogmatics III/2*" (Ph.D. diss., University of St Andrews, 2008).

63   Yong, *Theology and Down Syndrome*, 191. Michael Welker makes similar claims regarding the work of the Spirit. In his enumeration of the characteristics of the power of the Spirit, he notes that the Spirit "transforms and renews people and orders, and opens people to God's creative action." Furthermore, the Spirit "grants authority to the person who is publicly powerless, suffering, and

despised" and "enlists the services of this finite and perishable community, and changes and renews it in order to make God's power of creation and of new creation manifest and effective through and for this community." See Michael Welker, *God the Spirit* (Minneapolis: Augsburg Fortress, 1994), 220–21.

64   Dorothy Martyn offers a theological perspective on the origin of transformative qualities in therapeutic relationships. Martyn draws on Barth's dialectical statements regarding the qualities of God as "the One who loves in freedom"—the grace and holiness of God; the mercy and righteousness of God; and the patience and wisdom of God—to demonstrate the fact that caregivers are capable of offering this kind of care precisely because we have received it ourselves. She says, "For all of us, these qualities of relationship are not primary; they are mediated. Grace and holiness, mercy and righteousness, patience and wisdom are dependent on a higher source than humankind. There is something of receivership as the condition under which we can manifest any of them. We can turn in freely given, undeserved compassion only secondarily to having first been the recipient." See Martyn, *The Man in the Yellow Hat*, 192.

CHAPTER 4

1   John O'Brien and Connie Lyle O'Brien, "Learning to Listen," in *Little Book about Person-Centered Planning*, 15. Describing the kind of listening and collaboration necessary in person-centered work, the authors say, "We listen best when we stand with people; close enough to smell and hear each other, to touch and be touched. Standing with a person means being willing to accommodate the person's preferences for communicating, and being willing to thoughtfully consider joining the person in taking action. Habit tempts us to stand over or stand away from people with disabilities.... These habits take us away from the question we must need to answer. 'How can I show this person that I want to join her; that I want to be on her side in a constructive way[?'] Maybe I won't be able to help her do what she wants, but I want her to know that understanding what she wants matters to me."

2   Hunsinger, "Interdisciplinary Map," 218. Using the image of a traveler with a map, Hunsinger describes the need to make sense of the relationship between psychology and theology in her own ministry of pastoral counseling. She writes, "When I worked as a pastoral counselor, I often felt like I was traveling in uncharted territory.... I had various maps in hand, some constructed by depth psychologists and others drawn up by various theologians and spiritual guides, but how did they all fit together? If I followed one map only, we might find a clear path on which to travel, but would our destination be the one we had intended? Were all our efforts straining toward the kingdom of God or toward a more modest goal of healing from psychological trauma? Did the counselee long for the communion of saints or simply for relief from depression and loneliness? Were these different ways of conceiving of our destination compatible with each other, or would they take us in different directions?"

3   Hunsinger, "Interdisciplinary Map," 220.

4   Hunsinger, "Interdisciplinary Map," 221.
5   Hunsinger rightly emphasizes the important distinction between the Chalce-
    donian pattern and the Chalcedonian definition. She says, "The pattern merely
    provides form, whereas the definition is substantive. And because the pattern
    is formal, it can be applied to a variety of different relationships, whereas the
    substantive definition is specific to Christology. The pattern offers a kind of
    grammar, whereas the definition sets forth a particular statement in which the
    grammar is exemplified." See Hunsinger, "Interdisciplinary Map," 221. Barth
    employs this pattern throughout his *Church Dogmatics* as a means of considering
    the relationship between such concepts as divine and human agency, mystery and
    miracle, and soul and body. See Hunsinger, *How to Read Karl Barth*, 185–87.
6   Hunsinger, *Theology and Pastoral Counseling*, 231.
7   Hunsinger, *Theology and Pastoral Counseling*, 61–104.
8   Hunsinger, "Interdisciplinary Map," 225.
9   Shirley C. Guthrie Jr., "Pastoral Counseling, Trinitarian Theology, and Chris-
    tian Anthropology," *Interpretation* 33 (April 1979): 143. Cited in Hunsinger,
    Theology and Pastoral Counseling, 230–31. A pastoral caregiver's theological
    framework is operative in even the most nonparadigmatic pastoral friendship.
    Guthrie says, "Christian pastoral counseling motivated by a theology of grace
    will give up all neutrality about the goal of change, growth, or becoming. . . .
    Without manipulating people to attitudes and actions they do not freely choose
    for themselves, the counselor will openly stand for the Christian understanding
    of what fulfilled humanity looks like."
10 I was the chaplain at this facility. All names and identifying features of the pas-
    toral care receivers have been changed or omitted to preserve confidentiality.
    I am grateful to them, to their guardians, and to their facility for granting me
    permission to share their stories.
11 Anna Katherine Shurley, "Feeding Sheep," *Journal of Religion, Disability, and
    Health* 13, nos. 3–4 (2009): 333.
12 Winnicott, *Playing and Reality*, 86. Winnicott writes, "The patient on the couch
    or the child patient among the toys on the floor must be allowed to communicate
    a succession of ideas, thoughts, impulses, sensations that are not linked except
    in some way that is neurological or physiological and perhaps beyond detec-
    tion. . . . The therapist who cannot take this communication becomes engaged in
    a futile attempt to find some organization in the nonsense, as a result of which
    the patient leaves the nonsense area because of hopelessness about communicat-
    ing nonsense. An opportunity for rest has been missed because of the therapist's
    need to find sense where nonsense is" (74–75).
13 McNiff, *Art Heals*, 28.
14 It is important to note the challenge that comes with using the word "friend"
    in an institutional context. Bill and the chaplain considered themselves friends,
    yet the fact remained that the chaplain was an employee of the facility and thus
    subject to all the necessary boundaries that come with employment. The distinc-
    tion between the chaplain (an employee) and Bill (a resident and client) reflects

a common reality for many people with disabilities: often, their closest "friends" are also paid to be their support providers. This challenge cannot be overlooked. Even so, it is possible for a friendship to flourish between a person with a disability and someone who is paid to care for him or her.

15 Shurley, "Feeding Sheep," 333.

16 Christine Pohl, *Making Room: Recovering Hospitality as a Christian Tradition* (Grand Rapids: Eerdmans, 1999), 13.

17 Pohl, *Making Room*, 13.

18 Andrew D. Lester, *Anger: Discovering Your Spiritual Ally* (Louisville, Ky.: Westminster John Knox, 2007), 14.

19 Lester, *Anger*, 19.

20 Lester, *Anger*, 20.

21 Lester, *Anger*, 23–24.

22 The facility where Jerry lives is not equipped to make the kind of living accommodations (at group homes or at the main facility) that would be necessary if two residents were to marry. Furthermore, most of the facility's residents (including Jerry) are not their own guardians because they are not able to make life decisions for themselves. Therefore, marriage would simply not be possible for them.

23 Art therapist Shaun McNiff suggests that by participating in the creative process, people are able to engage in "a deep personal dialogue with images and feelings that instinctively present the needs of the soul." See McNiff, *Art Heals*, 19.

24 Andrew D. Lester, *The Angry Christian: A Theology for Care and Counseling* (Louisville, Ky.: Westminster John Knox, 2003), 8.

25 Lester, *Angry Christian*, 148–49. To fund his argument, Lester cites, for example, the Israelites' anger toward God as it is revealed in several of the Psalms. The Israelites very clearly express their anger while also conveying their faithfulness to the covenant. Lester suggests that "Expressing anger toward God may indeed be an act of honesty that restores authentic relationship with the divine" (141). Another example is found in Ephesians 4:26-27, where the author writes, "Be angry but do not sin." Here, Lester notes, the author "makes it clear that [he] is concerned about what we do with our anger" (144).

26 One of the essential elements of Lester's argument is drawn from recent neurological research suggesting that anger is "inherent to our embodied existence, part of our physical makeup that has been building on primitive brain systems for millions of years and did not just suddenly appear as if by mutation." See Lester, *Angry Christian*, 172. Thus, Lester believes that a pastoral theology of anger needs to be grounded in the doctrine of creation, not the doctrine of sin. Because the capacity for anger is part of the creation that God called good, we should consider it "a positive aspect of our selfhood." (176).

27 The care receiver chose her own pseudonym for this book. Her opportunity to choose proved to be another life-giving component of the person-centered care that transpired between the chaplain and the care receiver.

28 Warren explains, "It felt like a creative prank. I invited strangers to artistically share their deepest secret on a postcard and mail it to me, anonymously. . . .

The secrets come from all continents, in many languages, uncovering our inner diversity while reminding us of our deeper unity." See Frank Warren, *PostSecret: Confessions on Life, Death, and God* (New York: HarperCollins, 2009), 1.

29 Frank Warren started PostSecret with the hope of creating a "place where people could feel free to share their private hopes, desires, and fears—a place where the secrets they could not tell their friends and family would be treated with dignity and in a nonjudgmental way." See Guy Kawasaki, "Ten Questions with PostSecret's Frank Warren," *How to Change the World: A Practical Blog for Impractical People*, accessed September 20, 2011.

30 Gershen Kaufman, *Shame: The Power of Caring* (Rochester, Vt.: Schenkman Books, 1992), 8–9.

31 Neil Pembroke, *The Art of Listening: Dialogue, Shame, and Pastoral Care* (Edinburgh: T&T Clark/Handsel Press, 2002), 144–46.

32 James Fowler, *Faithful Change: The Personal and Public Challenges of Postmodern Life* (Nashville: Abingdon, 1996), 104–5.

33 Pearpoint and Forest, "Ethics of MAPS and PATH," 97.

34 Frederick Buechner, *Telling Secrets* (New York: HarperCollins, 1991), 2.

35 Barth, *Church Dogmatics*, vol. 3, pt. 2, 251.

36 O'Brien and O'Brien, "Learning to Listen," in *Little Book about Person-Centered Planning*, 16.

37 Deborah van Deusen Hunsinger, *Pray without Ceasing: Revitalizing Pastoral Care* (Grand Rapids: Eerdmans, 2006), 8.

38 Hunsinger, *Pray without Ceasing*, 9.

CHAPTER 5

1 John Swinton, *Building a Church for Strangers* (Edinburgh: Contact Pastoral Trust, 1999), 29.

2 Stanley Hauerwas and Charles Pinches, *Christians among the Virtues: Theological Conversations with Ancient and Modern Ethics* (South Bend, Ind.: University of Notre Dame Press, 1997), 49. "Christians must not only see friends as gifts to one another, they must see their friendship itself as a gift. They can do this precisely because they understand themselves to be actors within a story authored not by them but by God." Cited in Reinders, *Receiving the Gift of Friendship*, 366.

3 Amos Yong, *The Bible, Disability, and the Church: A New Vision for the People of God* (Grand Rapids: Eerdmans, 2011), 112. Yong asks, "What would happen if the public discovered that church communities were creating inclusive educational and liturgical environments because they valued the presence of children and people with intellectual disabilities? How might the mission of the church be reinvigorated precisely through having people with disabilities and their families in its midst? In what ways would the church be seen as more rather than less relevant to the world if it were to become a more hospitable community especially for people with intellectual disabilities?"

4 Yong, *Bible, Disability, and the Church*, 112.

5 Yong, *Bible, Disability, and the Church*, 111.

6   Barth, *Church Dogmatics*, vol. 4, pt. 3.2, 845.
7   Barth, *Church Dogmatics*, vol. 4, pt. 3.2, 809–10.
8   Barth, *Church Dogmatics*, vol. 4, pt. 3.2, 865–901.
9   Barth, *Church Dogmatics*, vol. 4, pt. 3.2, 885.
10 Barth, *Church Dogmatics*, vol. 4, pt. 3.2, 885. The Latin phrase *mutua consolatio fratrum* can be translated "the mutual consolation of the brethren." See Oswald Bayer, *Martin Luther's Theology: A Contemporary Interpretation*, trans. Thomas Trapp (Grand Rapids: Eerdmans, 2008), 277n103. Martin Luther understood this mutual conversation and consolation among Christian brothers and sisters to be part of the "office of the Word"—that is, the ministry entrusted to all baptized believers (not just the ordained) to proclaim God's saving work through Jesus Christ (257–58). Bayer cites one of Luther's sermons in which he speaks of this mutual ministry of care, saying, "Wherever even just one comes to another, there he should bring along comfort and deliverance. I should pour out my sadness to the one who is close to me and ask him for comfort. What that person promises to me as regards comfort is to be affirmed by God in heaven as well" (277).
11 Barth's description here of the practice of pastoral care in community does not include any reference to gladness, the fourth mark of an authentic human encounter. Nevertheless, Barth likely intends for the caring relationship to be a mutual interaction marked by gladness. If, in fact, the community's ministry is an act of witness to the work of God who, through Christ, has welcomed us into covenant partnership (friendship), then it stands to reason that our relationships with one another—especially our caring relationships, would be marked by gladness. When Christians interact with gladness, they demonstrate that they have claimed the secret of their humanity, namely that their freedom to interact with one another in the first place comes from the God who has welcomed them as friends. See Barth, *Church Dogmatics*, vol. 3, pt. 2, 265–67.
12 Since health, according to Barth, is "the strength to be as man" (*Church Dogmatics*, vol. 3, pt. 4, 356–57), healing can be understood as the restoration of the strength to live the life that God has given us—which includes living into our particular vocations.
13 Barth, *Church Dogmatics*, vol. 3, pt. 4, 899.
14 Barth, *Church Dogmatics*, vol. 3, pt. 4, 886.
15 John Swinton, *From Bedlam to Shalom: Towards a Practical Theology of Human Nature, Interpersonal Relationships, and Mental Health Care* (New York: Peter Lang, 2000), 43.
16 Swinton, *From Bedlam to Shalom*, 44.
17 Swinton, *From Bedlam to Shalom*, 45.
18 Swinton, *From Bedlam to Shalom*, 48.
19 Roy McCloughry and Wayne Morris, *Making a World of Difference: Christian Reflections on Disability* (London: SPCK, 2002), 121.
20 A church in Wisconsin, for example, established a care group for a woman named Kathy who had Down syndrome and wanted to become involved in the life of the congregation. The group engaged in fellowship activities and helped

Kathy with various personal and household tasks. Over the course of time, the group became a close-knit circle of friends that truly cared for one another, not just for Kathy. Kathy was no longer the focus of the group's work; she was a participant in their shared practices of caring. One member of the group recalls that during a particularly difficult time in her own life, Kathy contacted her and asked if she needed Kathy to start a circle of support for her. To this the woman responded, "You already have." See Lisa Pugh, prod., and John Schwartz, dir., *Believing, Belonging, Becoming: Stories of Faith Inclusion* (Madison: Wisconsin Council on Developmental Disabilities, 2002), film.

21 The supportive care group is a model for Christian pastoral care for people with disabilities and their families. Developed by a group of Mennonites in the 1980s, this model of care represents a response to the limitations of secular service providers. See Preheim-Bartel et al., *Supportive Care in the Congregation*.

22 Brett Webb-Mitchell likens this common attitude to that of the biblical character Martha. When Jesus comes to Martha's home for a visit, her focus is on accomplishing household tasks while her sister, Mary, sits with Jesus and gives him her undivided attention (Luke 10:38-42). Webb-Mitchell contends that, like Martha, church members often focus on caring for a person with a disability instead of being with them. See Brett Webb-Mitchell, "Teaching a Church to 'Be With': The Teamwork of God and John," in *Different Members, One Body: Welcoming the Diversity of Abilities in God's Family*, ed. Sharon Kutz-Mellem (Louisville, Ky.: Witherspoon Press, 1998), 58–59.

23 Pohl, *Making Room*, 71–72.

24 Pohl, *Making Room*, 157–58.

25 Jean Vanier, *Encountering "the Other"* (New York: Paulist, 2005), 12–13. Vanier writes, "Sometimes those of us who have more power, more money, more time or more knowledge bend down to those who have less power, less knowledge or less wealth; there is a movement from the 'superior' to the 'inferior'. . . . You can imagine someone in the street falling down and you going to help that person to get up. Then something happens. As you listen to that person you become friends. . . . You are not just being generous, you are entering into a relationship, which will change your life. You are no longer in control. You have become vulnerable; you have come to love that person. . . . In the heart of Christ there is a yearning to bring people together to meet as friends. To make that move from generosity to communion of hearts will imply a new way of living. It will imply a transformation, because we will have lost power."

26 In *A Place Called Acceptance*, Kathleen Deyer Bolduc shares an anonymous quotation from the father of a child with a disability who desires for a congregation to see his child as more than simply the recipient of care. The father says, "We need opportunities for genuine friendship and support, not pity or condescension. Most of all, we need [pastors and churches] to know that we have just as high expectations (albeit different) for our children as other parents, and want our children equipped to serve just like the others. . . . Many members of the church reflect society's attitudes—that we are to be pitied, that Johnny can't do

anything and must always be served." Kathleen Deyer Bolduc, *A Place Called Acceptance: Ministry with Families of Children with Disabilities* (Louisville, Ky.: Bridge Resources, 2001), 25.

27 Judith Snow, an author, artist, and advocate who lived with multiple disabilities, describes in her writing the kind contributions that people with disabilities can make to a community that will welcome and include them. She writes, "As fellow participants in an imperfect community many persons with disabilities have valuable gifts to offer. Some show a capacity to take a great deal of satisfaction from very simple everyday occurrences. The usual behavior of others can be a contribution to those who find society's restricted codes too tight for self-expression. The silent ones may be the best listeners. . . . There is an unlimited number of possible gifts that individually each person with a handicap can develop, like everyone, the nature of which can only be determined by those who stand close enough to watch, listen, care, and share. Welcoming into community those who have been excluded and recreating community so that these people's giftedness becomes part of everyday life—this is the strong road to building the capacity of communities everywhere." See Snow, "Power in Vulnerability," 12–13.

28 Jean Vanier addresses the importance of friendship in the lives of all people but especially those with disabilities. Drawing on his experience of members in the L'Arche community, Vanier says, "Today, some people idealize people with disabilities when they find autonomy, live alone, look at television and drink beer. Autonomy can be good to a certain extent, but in our community, a number of people who wanted to live alone fell into loneliness and alcoholism. The problem was not that they lived alone but that they lacked a network of friends. It always comes back to belonging. We have to discover more fully that the church is a place of compassion and fecundity, a place of welcome and friendship." See Stanley Hauerwas and Jean Vanier, *Living Gently in a Violent World: The Prophetic Witness of Weakness* (Downers Grove, Ill.: InterVarsity, 2008), 37.

29 Hauerwas and Vanier, *Living Gently*, 752.

30 Hauerwas and Vanier, *Living Gently*, 747.

31 Paul J. Wadell, *Becoming Friends: Worship, Justice, and the Practice of Christian Friendship* (Grand Rapids: Brazos, 2002), 40.

32 Bill Gaventa challenges this implication with a series of helpful questions. He asks, "Is their vocation that of helping other people to understand what it means to be human, to come to terms with our projections, illusions, and self-deceptions, and to come into deeper and closer relationships with others and with God? If so, are they valued and compensated for that role? What if they want to contribute or serve in other ways that have nothing to do with my transformation? Is that why we celebrate them? The reason I bring this up as a caveat is that I have had people with disabilities tell me that they would prefer that I not use them to work out my own issues." See William C. Gaventa, "Learning from People with Disabilities: How to Ask the Right Questions," in *The Paradox of Disability: Responses*

to Jean Vanier and L'Arche Communities from Theology and the Sciences, ed. Hans Reinders (Grand Rapids: Eerdmans, 2010), 107.

33   Hunsinger, *Pray without Ceasing*, 1–3.

34   Hunsinger, *Pray without Ceasing*, 13.

35   Hunsinger, *Pray without Ceasing*, 13.

36   John Swinton describes Christian friendship as "catalytic." He says, "Unlike other more instrumental relationships such as those found in counseling and psychotherapy, which set out specifically to do something, it is a form of relationship that acts as a catalyst that enables health and rehumanization simply by being there. . . . The task of the Christlike friend is not to do anything for them, but rather to be someone for them—someone who understands and accepts them as persons; someone who is with and for them in the way that God is also with and for them; someone who reveals the nature of God and the transforming power of the Spirit of Christ in a form that is tangible, accessible, deeply powerful." See Swinton, *Resurrecting the Person: Friendship and the Care of People with Mental Health Problems* (Nashville: Abingdon, 2000), 143.

37   Hans Reinders addresses the importance of the Church's embracing friendship with people with intellectual disabilities, noting the ways that it is a source of transformation for the Church and its members. He says, "Every human being is worthy of being chosen as a friend simply because that is what God does—choose us to be friends. We need friendship if we are to flourish as human beings. The theological justification for this claim is that friendship with our fellow creatures is our vocation. This is what we were created for. . . . People with intellectual disabilities, let alone profound intellectual disabilities, do not fit easily within our conceptions of the good life. That's what the focus on friendship is meant to show, not only in a critical sense but also in a constructive sense. I want Christians to consider friendship with a disabled person as a vocation that, once they have entered into it, will change not only their own lives but also the life of the church." See Reinders, *Receiving the Gift of Friendship*, 162–63. Reinders is not suggesting that people with intellectual disabilities are somehow useful to us, but instead is encouraging the Church to recognize and receive friendship with all people as a gift in itself.

38   In recent years, a number of authors have developed resources for congregations desiring to become more inclusive of people with physical and intellectual disabilities. See, for example, Ann Rose Davie and Ginny Thornburgh, *That All May Worship: An Interfaith Welcome to People with Disabilities* (Washington, D.C.: National Organization on Disability, 1994); Janet Miller Rife and Ginny Thornburgh, *From Barriers to Bridges: A Community Action Guide for Congregations and People with Disabilities* (Washington, D.C.: National Organization on Disability, 1996); Bolduc, *A Place Called Acceptance*; and Sharon Kutz-Mellem, ed., *Different Members, One Body: Welcoming the Diversity of Abilities in God's Family* (Louisville, Ky.: Witherspoon Press, 1998).

39   Erik W. Carter, *Including People with Disabilities in Faith Communities: A Guide for Service Providers, Families, and Congregations* (Baltimore: Paul H. Brookes Publishing, 2007), 28.

40   Davie and Thornburgh, *That All May Worship*, 45–46.

41   Davie and Thornburgh, *That All May Worship*, 6.

42   Carter, *Including People with Disabilities*, 29.

43   Carter, *Including People with Disabilities*, 33–38.

44   The field of health ministry attests to the Church's capacity to address the health-care needs of people within and beyond its membership. See, for example, Abigail Rian Evans, *The Healing Church: Practical Programs for Health Ministries* (Cleveland: United Church Press, 1999) and Mary Chase-Ziolek, *Health, Healing, and Wholeness: Engaging Congregations in Ministries of Health* (Cleveland: Pilgrim Press, 2005).

45   Rabbi Joseph Potasnik warns, "Being present does not mean being included." See Rabbi Joseph Potasnik, video interview, in *A Place for All: Faith and Community for Persons with Disabilities* (Diva Communications, 2009), film.

46   William C. Gaventa, video interview, in *A Place for All*.

47   Bruce Anderson, *Our Door Is Open: Creating Welcoming Cultures in Helping Organizations* (Vashon, Wash.: Community Activators, 2010), audio presentation.

48   Anderson, *Our Door Is Open*. A powerful example of this can be seen in the recent award-winning documentary *Praying with Lior*. This film follows Lior Liebling, a young Jewish boy, and his family as they prepare for Lior's bar mitzvah. Lior has a strong, compelling faith that has influenced members of his faith community for the better. For example, one member of Lior's congregation acknowledges that she has moments during their corporate davening (praying) when she becomes distracted and loses her focus. When these moments occur, she says that she turns to Lior, who is always praying with his whole heart, and she becomes centered again. See Ilana Trachtman, dir., *Praying with Lior* (New York: First Run Features, 2007), film.

49   Carter, *Including People with Disabilities*, 75. This kind of pastoral friendship is also a central component of the ministry of Bridges to Faith, an organization in Massachusetts devoted to helping people with disabilities participate in faith communities. In this ministry, a person from a faith community is invited to become a "faith companion" for a person with a disability, entering into friendship with him or her and facilitating involvement in the life of the congregation. This kind of friendship is significant for everyone involved: "For the individual we refer this offers an opportunity not only to have spiritual needs met but also provides a sense of belonging, friendship and value not easily obtained. For congregations this becomes an opportunity to participate in a genuine ministry of love which enhances their whole life and spirit." See Bridges to Faith, "Faith Companions," accessed February 14, 2012, www.bridgestofaith.org.

50   Carter, *Including People with Disabilities*, 75. Erik Carter describes the relationship between Samantha, a woman with an intellectual disability, and Ellen, a fellow member of Samantha's faith community. He says, "When Samantha first

began attending church at St. Mark's she and Ellen decided to be faith partners. They sat together each week during worship services and Ellen helped Samantha follow along as they sang from the hymnal, recited the responsive reading, and read passages of scripture. Ellen occasionally provided whispered explanations of certain aspects of the worship service so that Samantha knew exactly what to expect. Together, they composed and rehearsed a prayer that Samantha later shared with the congregation. In addition, Ellen always read the bulletin aloud to keep Samantha informed of upcoming church events, asking her about activities in which she might like to participate. When Ellen was sick, Samantha was the first person asking others for prayer."

51 Hunsinger, *Pray without Ceasing*, xiii. Deborah Hunsinger's vision of pastoral care groups is compatible with the notion of pastoral friendship groups, as both nurture the koinonia that is the heart of pastoral care and operate according to the assumption that "our deepest need—which offers the vital cure—is for God and one another" (194).

52 Hunsinger, *Pray without Ceasing*, 194–96. Hunsinger offers several examples of pastoral care groups with different purposes. As with pastoral care groups, pastoral friendship groups may differ in purpose. Given the "variety of gifts" that are found within faith communities and among its members with intellectual disabilities, it stands to reason that, for example, one person with an intellectual disability may desire to be part of a group whose purpose is to pray for people who are in need of healing, while another person with an intellectual disability may desire to participate in a group focused on discerning God's call to the community and its individual members (194).

53 Hunsinger, *Pray without Ceasing*, 196–97.

54 Hunsinger, *Pray without Ceasing*, 197.

55 My thanks to Bill Gaventa for introducing me to this resource for pastoral care with people with intellectual disabilities.

56 Paul Bosch, worship ed., "Worship Supplement," *CIRCLE* (1974).

57 Hunsinger, *Pray without Ceasing*, 199.

58 Niles Borop, "Blest Be the Tie," in *The Baptist Hymnal*, ed. Wesley L. Forbis (Nashville: Convention Press, 1991), 387.

59 Craig Dykstra and Dorothy C. Bass, "Times of Yearning, Practices of Faith," in *Practicing our Faith: A Way of Life for a Searching People*, ed. Dorothy C. Bass (San Francisco: Jossey-Bass, 1997), 5. In an earlier article, Craig Dykstra challenges the view that "practices" are something done *to* and *for* others and argues that Christian practices are, fundamentally, things we do *with* one another. See Craig Dykstra, "Reconceiving Practice," in *Shifting Boundaries: Contextual Approaches to the Structure of Theological Education*, ed. Barbara Wheeler and Edward Farley (Louisville, Ky.: Westminster John Knox, 1991), 47–48. Cited in Hunsinger, *Pray without Ceasing*, xi.

Bibliography

American Association on Intellectual and Developmental Disabilities. "Frequently Asked Questions on Intellectual Disability." Accessed March 2, 2017. http://aaidd.org/intellectual-disability/definition/faqs-on-intellectual-disability.

———. "Frequently Asked Questions on Intellectual Disabilities and the AAIDD Definition." 2008. Accessed March 2, 2017. https://aaidd.org/docs/default-source/sis-docs/aaiddfaqonid_template.pdf.

Anderson, Bruce. *Our Door Is Open: Creating Welcoming Cultures in Helping Organizations.* Vashon, Wash.: Community Activators, 2010. Audio Presentation.

Barth, Karl. *Church Dogmatics.* Vol. 1, pt. 1, *The Doctrine of the Word of God.* Edinburgh: T&T Clark, 1975.

———. *Church Dogmatics.* Vol. 2, pt. 1, *The Doctrine of God.* Edinburgh: T&T Clark, 1957.

———. *Church Dogmatics.* Vol. 3, pt. 2, *The Doctrine of Creation.* London: T&T Clark, 2004.

———. *Church Dogmatics.* Vol. 3, pt. 4, *The Doctrine of Creation.* London: T&T Clark, 2004.

———. *Church Dogmatics.* Vol. 4, pt. 2, *The Doctrine of Reconciliation.* London: T&T Clark, 2004.

———. *Church Dogmatics.* Vol. 4, pt. 3.2, *The Doctrine of Reconciliation.* London: T&T Clark, 2004.

Bayer, Oswald. *Martin Luther's Theology: A Contemporary Interpretation.* Translated by Thomas Trapp. Grand Rapids: Eerdmans, 2008.

Block, Jennie Weiss. *Copious Hosting: A Theology of Access for People with Disabilities*. New York: Continuum, 2002.

Bolduc, Kathleen Deyer. *A Place Called Acceptance: Ministry with Families of Children with Disabilities*. Louisville, Ky.: Bridge Resources, 2001.

Borop, Niles. "Blest Be the Tie." In *The Baptist Hymnal*, edited by Wesley L. Forbis. Nashville: Convention Press, 1991.

Bosch, Paul, worship editor. "Worship Supplement." *CIRCLE* (1974).

Bridges to Faith. "Faith Companions." Accessed February 14, 2012. www.bridgestofaith.org.

Buechner, Frederick. *Telling Secrets*. New York: HarperCollins, 1991.

Callahan, Daniel. "The WHO Definition of 'Health.'" *Hastings Center Studies* 1, no. 3 (1973): 77–87. Reprinted in *On Moral Medicine: Theological Perspectives in Medical Ethics*, edited by Stephen E. Lammers and Allen Verhey. 2nd ed. Grand Rapids: Eerdmans, 1998.

Caprio-Orsini, Cindy. *A Thousand Words: Healing Through Art for People with Developmental Disabilities*. Quebec: Diverse City Press, 1996.

Carter, Erik W. *Including People with Disabilities in Faith Communities: A Guide for Service Providers, Families, and Congregations*. Baltimore: Paul H. Brookes Publishing, 2007.

Chase-Ziolek, Mary. *Health, Healing, and Wholeness: Engaging Congregations in Ministries of Health*. Cleveland: Pilgrim Press, 2005.

Collins, Francis. Foreword to *Playing God? Genetic Determinism and Human Freedom*, by Ted Peters. New York: Routledge, 1997.

Conner, Benjamin T. *Amplifying Our Witness: Giving Voice to Adolescents with Developmental Disabilities*. Grand Rapids: Eerdmans, 2012.

Davie, Ann Rose, and Ginny Thornburgh. *That All May Worship: An Interfaith Welcome to People with Disabilities*. Washington, D.C.: National Organization on Disability, 1994.

Demmons, Tracy. "Being in Encounter: Toward a Post-critical Theology of the Knowledge of God for Persons with Intellectual Disabilities: With Special Reference to Karl Barth's *Church Dogmatics III/2*." Ph.D. diss., University of St Andrews, 2008.

de Vinck, Christopher. *The Power of the Powerless*. New York: Doubleday, 1988.

Doerfler, Walter. "*Conditio Humana* as Viewed by a Geneticist." In *Theology, Disability and the New Genetics: Why Science Needs the Church*, edited by John Swinton and Brian Brock. New York: T&T Clark, 2007.

Dollar, Ellen Painter. *No Easy Choice: Disability, Parenthood, and Faith in an Age of Advanced Reproduction.* Louisville, Ky.: Westminster John Knox, 2012.

Dykstra, Craig. "Reconceiving Practice." In *Shifting Boundaries: Contextual Approaches to the Structure of Theological Education,* edited by Barbara Wheeler and Edward Farley. Louisville, Ky.: Westminster John Knox, 1991.

Dykstra, Craig, and Dorothy C. Bass. "Times of Yearning, Practices of Faith." In *Practicing our Faith: A Way of Life for a Searching People,* edited by Dorothy C. Bass. San Francisco: Jossey-Bass, 1997.

Eiesland, Nancy. *The Disabled God: Toward a Liberatory Theology of Disability.* Nashville: Abingdon, 1994.

Evans, Abigail Rian. *The Healing Church: Practical Programs for Health Ministries.* Cleveland: United Church Press, 1999.

Falvey, Mary, Marsha Forest, Jack Pearpoint, and Richard Rosenberg. *All My Life's a Circle: Using the Tools—Circles, MAPS and PATHS.* Toronto: Inclusion Press, 1997.

Fife, Robert, and Jim Pierson. "A Model of Compassion: The Role of the Church for Persons Having Disabilities." In *Reaching Out to Special People: A Resource for Ministry with Persons Who Have Disabilities,* edited by Jim Pierson and Robert Korth. Cincinnati: Standard Publishing, 1989.

Fowler, James. *Faithful Change: The Personal and Public Challenges of Postmodern Life.* Nashville: Abingdon, 1996.

Gaventa, William C. "Bring On the Church Coach!" *Disability Solutions* 1, no. 4 (1996): 1, 3.

———. "Creating and Energizing Caring Communities." In *Caregiving and Loss: Family Needs, Professional Responses,* edited by Kenneth J. Doka and Joyce Davidson. Washington, D.C.: Hospice Foundation of America, 2003.

———. "Learning from People with Disabilities: How to Ask the Right Questions." In *The Paradox of Disability: Responses to Jean Vanier and L'Arche Communities from Theology and the Sciences,* edited by Hans Reinders. Grand Rapids: Eerdmans, 2010.

———. Video interview. In *A Place for All: Faith and Community for Persons with Disabilities.* Diva Communications, 2009. Film.

Guthrie, Shirley C., Jr. "Pastoral Counseling, Trinitarian Theology, and Christian Anthropology." *Interpretation* 33 (1979): 130–43.

Hall, Amy Laura. *Conceiving Parenthood: American Protestantism and the Spirit of Reproduction*. Grand Rapids: Eerdmans, 2008.

Hauerwas, Stanley. *Sanctify Them in the Truth: Holiness Exemplified*. Nashville: Abingdon, 1998.

Hauerwas, Stanley, and Charles Pinches. *Christians among the Virtues: Theological Conversations with Ancient and Modern Ethics*. South Bend, Ind.: University of Notre Dame Press, 1997.

Hauerwas, Stanley, and Jean Vanier. *Living Gently in a Violent World: The Prophetic Witness of Weakness*. Downers Grove, Ill.: InterVarsity, 2008.

Hunsinger, Deborah van Deusen. "An Interdisciplinary Map for Christian Counselors: Theology and Psychology in Pastoral Counseling." In *Care for the Soul*, edited by Mark McMinn and Timothy Phillips. Downers Grove, Ill.: InterVarsity, 2001.

———. *Pray without Ceasing: Revitalizing Pastoral Care*. Grand Rapids: Eerdmans, 2006.

———. *Theology and Pastoral Counseling: A New Interdisciplinary Approach*. Grand Rapids: Eerdmans, 1995.

Hunsinger, George. *How to Read Karl Barth: The Shape of His Theology*. New York: Oxford University Press, 1991.

———. "The Mediator of Communion." In *Disruptive Grace: Studies in the Theology of Karl Barth*. Grand Rapids: Eerdmans, 2000.

Kaufman, Gershen. *Shame: The Power of Caring*. Rochester, Vt.: Schenkman Books, 1992.

Kawasaki, Guy. "Ten Questions with PostSecret's Frank Warren." *How to Change the World: A Practical Blog for Impractical People*. Accessed September 20, 2011. https://guykawasaki.com/ten-questions-w-2/.

Korth, Robert E. "Your Special Friends: Misconceptions, Temptations, and Surprises in Ministry with Adults Having Mental Retardation." In *Reaching Out to Special People: A Resource for Ministry with Persons Who Have Disabilities*, edited by Jim Pierson and Robert Korth. Cincinnati: Standard Publishing, 1989.

Kugel, Robert. "Why Innovative Action?" In *Changing Patterns in Residential Services for the Mentally Retarded*, edited by Robert Kugel and Wolf Wolfensberger. Washington, D.C.: President's Committee on Mental Retardation, U.S. Printing Office, 1969.

Kutz-Mellem, Sharon, ed. *Different Members, One Body: Welcoming the Diversity of Abilities in God's Family*. Louisville, Ky.: Witherspoon Press, 1998.

Kuzmič, Rhys. "*Beruf* and *Berufung* in Karl Barth's *Church Dogmatics*: Toward a Subversive Klesiology." *International Journal of Systematic Theology* 7, no. 3 (2005): 262–78.

Lester, Andrew D. *Anger: Discovering Your Spiritual Ally*. Louisville, Ky.: Westminster John Knox, 2007.

————. *The Angry Christian: A Theology for Care and Counseling*. Louisville, Ky.: Westminster John Knox, 2003.

Leidy, Peter. "Whose Life Is It Anyway?" In *Make a Difference: A Guidebook for Person-Centered Direct Support*, by John O'Brien and Beth Mount. Toronto: Inclusion Press, 2005.

Linton, Simi. "Reassigning Meaning." In *The Disability Studies Reader*, edited by Lennard J. Davis. 2nd ed. New York: Routledge, 2006.

Loder, James. *The Logic of the Spirit: Human Development in Theological Perspective*. San Francisco: Jossey-Bass, 1998.

Maddocks, Morris. *The Christian Healing Ministry*. London: SPCK, 1990.

Mahowald, Mary B. "Aren't We All Eugenicists Anyway?" In *Theology, Disability and the New Genetics: Why Science Needs the Church*, edited by John Swinton and Brian Brock. New York: T&T Clark, 2007.

Martyn, Dorothy. *The Man in the Yellow Hat: Theology and Psychoanalysis in Child Therapy*. Atlanta: Scholars Press, 1992.

McCloughry, Roy, and Wayne Morris. *Making a World of Difference: Christian Reflections on Disability*. London: SPCK, 2002.

McKenny, Gerald P. *To Relieve the Human Condition: Bioethics, Technology, and the Body*. Albany: State University of New York Press, 1997.

McNiff, Shaun. *Art Heals: How Creativity Cures the Soul*. Boston: Shambhala Publications, 2004.

Mikkelsen, Hans Vium. *Reconciling Humanity: Karl Barth in Dialogue*. Grand Rapids: Eerdmans, 2010.

Modahl, Craig. "Finding a Place at the Table." *Journal of Religion, Disability and Health* 13, nos. 3–4 (2009): 320–22.

Moltmann, Jürgen. *The Source of Life: The Holy Spirit and the Theology of Life*. Minneapolis: Fortress, 1997.

Mount, Beth. "The Art and Soul of Person-Centered Planning." In *Implementing Person-Centered Planning: Voices of Experience*, edited by John O'Brien and Connie Lyle O'Brien. Toronto: Inclusion Press, 2002.

National Council of Churches, USA. "Fearfully and Wonderfully Made: A Policy on Human Biotechnologies Adopted November 2006." Accessed February 7, 2012. www.nccusa.org/pdfs/adoptedpolicy.pdf.

Newell, Christopher. "'What's Wrong with You?' Disability and Genes as Ethics." In *Theology, Disability and the New Genetics: Why Science Needs the Church*, edited by John Swinton and Brian Brock. New York: T&T Clark, 2007.

Nirje, Bengt. "The Normalization Principle and Its Human Management Implications." In *Changing Patterns in Residential Services for the Mentally Retarded*, edited by Robert Kugel and Wolf Wolfensberger. Washington, D.C.: President's Committee on Mental Retardation, U.S. Printing Office, 1969.

Nouwen, Henri. Introduction to *The Power of the Powerless*, by Christopher de Vinck. New York: Doubleday, 1988.

O'Brien, John, and Beth Mount. *Make a Difference: A Guidebook for Person-Centered Direct Support.* Toronto: Inclusion Press, 2005.

O'Brien, John, and Connie Lyle O'Brien, eds. *Implementing Person-Centered Planning: Voices of Experience.* Toronto: Inclusion Press, 2002.

———. "Learning to Listen." In *A Little Book about Person-Centered Planning*, edited by John O'Brien and Connie Lyle O'Brien. Toronto: Inclusion Press, 1998.

———. *A Little Book about Person-Centered Planning.* Toronto: Inclusion Press, 1998.

———. "The Origins of Person-Centered Planning: A Community of Practice Perspective." In *Implementing Person-Centered Planning: Voices of Experience*, edited by John O'Brien and Connie Lyle O'Brien. Toronto: Inclusion Press, 2002.

Pearpoint, Jack, and Marsha Forest. "The Ethics of MAPS and PATH." In *A Little Book about Person-Centered Planning*, edited by John O'Brien and Connie Lyle O'Brien. Toronto: Inclusion Press, 1998.

Pembroke, Neil. *The Art of Listening: Dialogue, Shame, and Pastoral Care.* Edinburgh: T&T Clark/Handsel Press, 2002.

Perske, Robert. "An Attempt to Find an Adequate Theological View of Mental Retardation." In *The Pastoral Voice of Robert Perske*, edited by William C. Gaventa and David L. Coulter. New York: Haworth Press, 2003.

Pierson, Jim. "Introduction: Close Enough to Notice." In *Reaching Out to Special People: A Resource for Ministry with Persons Who Have Disabilities*, edited by Jim Pierson and Robert Korth. Cincinnati: Standard Publishing, 1989.

Pohl, Christine. *Making Room: Recovering Hospitality as a Christian Tradition.* Grand Rapids: Eerdmans, 1999.

Potasnik, Rabbi Joseph. Video interview. In *A Place for All: Faith and Community for Persons with Disabilities*. Diva Communications, 2009. Film.

Preheim-Bartel, Dean, Aldred Neufeldt, Paul Leichty, and Christine Guth. *Supportive Care in the Congregation: Providing a Congregational Network of Care for Persons with Significant Disabilities*. Rev. ed. Goshen, Ind.: Mennonite Publishing Network, 2011.

President's Committee for People with Intellectual Disabilities. "Fact Sheet." Accessed November 14, 2009. http://www.acf.hhs.gov/programs/pcpid/pcpid_fact.html.

Price, Daniel. *Karl Barth's Anthropology in Light of Modern Thought*. Grand Rapids: Eerdmans, 2002.

Pugh, Lisa, prod., and John Schwartz, dir. *Believing, Belonging, Becoming: Stories of Faith Inclusion*. Madison: Wisconsin Council on Developmental Disabilities, 2002. Film.

Race, David, ed. *Leadership and Change in Human Services: Selected Readings from Wolf Wolfensberger*. London: Routledge, 2003.

Reinders, Hans. *The Future of the Disabled in Liberal Society: An Ethical Analysis*. South Bend, Ind.: University of Notre Dame Press, 2000.

———. "Life's Goodness: On Disability, Genetics and 'Choice.'" In *Theology, Disability and the New Genetics: Why Science Needs the Church*, edited by John Swinton and Brian Brock. New York: T&T Clark, 2007.

———. *Receiving the Gift of Friendship: Profound Disability, Theological Anthropology, and Ethics*. Grand Rapids: Eerdmans, 2008.

Reynolds, Thomas. *Vulnerable Communion: A Theology of Disability and Hospitality*. Grand Rapids: Brazos, 2008.

Rife, Janet Miller, and Ginny Thornburgh. *From Barriers to Bridges: A Community Action Guide for Congregations and People with Disabilities*. Washington, D.C.: National Organization on Disability, 1996.

Ritchie, Pete. "A Turn for the Better." In *Implementing Person-Centered Planning: Voices of Experience*, edited by John O'Brien and Connie Lyle O'Brien. Toronto: Inclusion Press, 2002.

Rizzuto, Ana-Maria. *The Birth of the Living God: A Psychoanalytic Study*. Chicago: University of Chicago Press, 1979.

Rosato, Philip J. *The Spirit as Lord: The Pneumatology of Karl Barth*. Edinburgh: T&T Clark, 1981.

Shuman, Joel James, and Keith G. Meador. *Heal Thyself: Spirituality, Medicine, and the Distortion of Christianity*. New York: Oxford University Press, 2003.

Shurley, Anna Katherine. "Feeding Sheep." *Journal of Religion, Disability, and Health* 13, nos. 3–4 (2009): 331–33.

Smith, Blair. "Researching Genetics and Health: Implications for Public Health Primary Care Medicine." In *Theology, Disability and the New Genetics: Why Science Needs the Church*, edited by John Swinton and Brian Brock. New York: T&T Clark, 2007.

Snow, Judith. "The Power in Vulnerability." In *A Little Book about Person-Centered Planning*, edited by John O'Brien and Connie Lyle O'Brien. Toronto: Inclusion Press, 1998.

Swinton, John. *Building a Church for Strangers*. Edinburgh: Contact Pastoral Trust, 1999.

———. *From Bedlam to Shalom: Towards a Practical Theology of Human Nature, Interpersonal Relationships, and Mental Health Care*. New York: Peter Lang, 2000.

———. "Introduction: Reimagining Genetics and Disability." In *Theology, Disability and the New Genetics: Why Science Needs the Church*, edited by John Swinton and Brian Brock. New York: T&T Clark, 2007.

———. *Resurrecting the Person: Friendship and the Care of People with Mental Health Problems*. Nashville: Abingdon, 2000.

Swinton, John, and Brian Brock, eds. *Theology, Disability and the New Genetics: Why Science Needs the Church*. New York: T&T Clark, 2007.

Tomilio, Joseph, III. "Called by Grace: Elucidating and Appropriating the Doctrine of Vocation in Karl Barth's Church Dogmatics." *The New Mercersburg Review* 34 (2004): 3–11.

Trachtman, Ilana, dir. *Praying with Lior*. New York: First Run Features, 2007. Film.

Ulanov, Ann Belford. *Finding Space: God, Winnicott, and Psychic Reality*. Louisville, Ky.: Westminster John Knox, 2001.

Ulanov, Ann Belford, and Alvin Dueck. *The Living God and Our Living Psyche: What Christians Can Learn from Carl Jung*. Grand Rapids: Eerdmans, 2008.

Ulanov, Ann, and Barry Ulanov. *The Healing Imagination: The Meeting of Psyche and Soul*. Mahwah, N.J.: Paulist, 1991.

Vanier, Jean. *Becoming Human*. New York: Paulist, 1998.

———. *Community and Growth*. London: Darton, Longman & Todd, 1989.

———. *Encountering "the Other."* New York: Paulist, 2005.

Wadell, Paul J. *Becoming Friends: Worship, Justice, and the Practice of Christian Friendship*. Grand Rapids: Brazos, 2002.

Warren, Frank. *PostSecret: Confessions on Life, Death, and God.* New York: HarperCollins, 2009.

Webb-Mitchell, Brett. *Beyond Accessibility: Toward Full Inclusion of People with Disabilities in Faith Communities.* New York: Church Publishing International, 2010.

———. *Dancing with Disabilities: Opening the Church to All God's Children.* Cleveland: United Church Press, 1996.

———. "Teaching a Church to 'Be With': The Teamwork of God and John." In *Different Members, One Body: Welcoming the Diversity of Abilities in God's Family,* edited by Sharon Kutz-Mellem. Louisville, Ky.: Witherspoon Press, 1998.

Welker, Michael. *God the Spirit.* Minneapolis: Augsburg Fortress, 1994.

"WHO Definition of Health." Preamble to the constitution of the World Health Organization as adopted by the International Health Conference, New York, June 19–22, 1946. Signed June 22, 1946. Entered into force April 7, 1948.

Winnicott, D. W. "The Capacity to Be Alone." In *The Maturational Processes and the Facilitating Environment.* Madison: International Universities Press, 1965.

———. "Ego Distortion in Terms of True and False Self." In *The Maturational Processes and the Facilitating Environment.* Madison: International Universities Press, 1965.

———. "Ego Integration in Child Development." In *The Maturational Processes and the Facilitating Environment.* Madison: International Universities Press, 1965.

———. *Human Nature.* New York: Schocken Books, 1988.

———. "Paediatrics and Psychiatry." In *Through Paediatrics to Psychoanalysis.* New York: Basic Books, 1975.

———. *Playing and Reality.* London: Routledge, 2006.

———. "Primary Maternal Preoccupation." In *Through Paediatrics to Psycho-analysis.* New York: Basic Books, 1975.

———. "The Theory of the Parent-Infant Relationship." In *The Maturational Processes and the Facilitating Environment.* Madison: International Universities Press, 1965.

Wolfensberger, Wolf. *Normalization: The Principle of Normalization in Human Services.* Toronto: National Institute on Mental Retardation, 1972.

———. Excerpt from "The Bad Things That Typically Get Done to Devalued People." In *Leadership and Change in Human Services:*

Selected Readings from Wolf Wolfensberger, edited by David Race. London: Routledge, 2003.

Yong, Amos. *The Bible, Disability, and the Church: A New Vision for the People of God*. Grand Rapids: Eerdmans, 2011.

———. *Theology and Down Syndrome: Reimagining Disability in Late Modernity*. Waco, Tex.: Baylor University Press, 2007.

Index

agape, 57, 88, 94, 122n55
anger, 74–77, 126n25, 126n26
art, coloring, 31, 66–69, 85

balance of power, 33
being with, 93
belonging, 9, 105, 130n28, 132n49
body, 35, 48, 53, 72, 74, 80, 107n1,
    116n45; of Christ, 93–95, 97, 103–
    4, 112n37, 119n29; and soul, 56,
    113n43, 122n52, 122n53, 123n55,
    125n5; theology, 87

calling, 7, 16, 46–48, 55, 88, 94, 101,
    104, 110n17, 117n8; obedience to,
    49–50, 85; *telos* of, 49, 84
capabilities, 14, 16, 47, 92
capacity thinking, 14, 100
caring ministry, 8, 92, 95–96
Chalcedonian pattern: approach,
    23, 63; definition, 63; general, 22,
    113n43, 113n45, 125n5
church, 3–4, 6–9, 18–24, 27, 42, 46,
    50, 60, 62–64, 87–93, 101, 103–5,
    113n41, 119n27, 119n29, 127n3,
    128n20, 129n22, 129n26, 130n28,
    131n37, 132n44, 133n50
circle of support, 14, 37, 46, 112n31,
    129n20
co-humanity, 52–57, 70–71, 77, 82,
    84, 90
collaboration, 8, 11, 16, 23, 28–31,
    34, 36, 38, 43, 46, 58, 61–62, 64,
    68, 70–71, 77, 84, 95, 124n1
community, 3, 5–8, 12, 14–15, 17,
    19–20, 24, 27–29, 35–36, 39, 45–
    46, 59, 63, 67, 69, 77, 81, 87–95,
    97–100, 102, 104, 110n18, 113n41,
    123n55, 124n63, 127n3, 128n11,
    127n27, 130n28, 132n49, 132n50,
    133n52
compliance, 32, 35, 115n25
congregation, 6–7, 18–21, 90, 97–
    100, 103, 128n20, 129n26, 131n38,
    132n48, 132n49, 133n50
creative living, 35–36, 115n24,
    115n25
creativity, 8, 28, 31–32, 34–36,
    38, 46, 48, 54, 100, 102, 115n24,
    115n25, 115n27
cure of souls, 89–90, 92, 113n41

145

deep listening, 24, 39, 61, 95

desires, 8, 15, 24, 27, 34–35, 80–81, 83, 127n29

deVinck, Christopher, 45

direct support, 37–39, 72, 115n35

disability: developmental, 71, 78–79; general, 4, 6–8, 12, 17, 41–42, 45, 51, 53, 61, 70–72, 74–76, 78–82, 84, 87–88, 93, 94, 100, 105, 107n1, 108n9, 112n31, 114n10, 115n35, 122n53, 126n14, 129n22, 129n26, 132n49; intellectual, 1, 4, 5, 7, 9, 11, 17, 36, 46–47, 50–51, 53–54, 57–58, 71, 78, 85, 102–5, 109n2, 109n4, 119n29, 121n39, 132n50, 133n52; services, 8, 12, 13, 37, 58; supports, 13–14, 21

disease, 4, 17, 107n1, 111n24

Down syndrome, 5, 108n9, 128n20

dreams, 8, 11–12, 15, 17–18, 23–24, 28, 31–32, 34, 36, 37–40, 42–44, 46, 57–62, 74–75, 78, 80–83, 85, 95–97, 100, 105

empower, 4, 8, 9, 13, 15, 17, 20, 21, 28, 35, 38, 49, 58, 61, 67, 90, 91; by Holy Spirit, 56, 94, 122n53

eugenics, 5, 107n1, 108n7

faithfulness, 3, 18, 46, 48, 50–51, 55, 62, 100, 126n25

faith partners, 100, 133n50

false self, 32–35, 39

fear, 5, 9, 32, 39, 50, 56, 80, 82, 85, 96, 104, 127n29

fellowship, 55, 77, 88, 89, 95, 98, 103–4, 118n19, 119n21, 123n55, 128n20

friendship: general, 2–4, 6, 8–9, 20, 57–58, 66, 69, 70–71, 82, 84, 87, 91, 93–95, 97, 99–100, 104, 126n14, 127n2, 128n11, 129n26, 130n28, 131n36, 131n37; pastoral, 46–47, 49, 57–59, 61–65, 70, 78, 82–85, 88, 90–92, 94–97, 99–100, 104–5, 125n9, 132n49; with God, 40, 47–49, 50–51, 57–58, 64, 84, 88, 95–96, 99

genetics: disorders, 5, 108n9; research, 4, 107n1

gladness, 55–56, 70, 77–78, 85, 94–95, 105, 128n11

good-enough care, 29–32, 34, 36, 39–40

gospel, 9, 16, 45, 88–89, 98, 118n10, 121n39

healing, 104, 113n43, 114n6, 124n2, 118n16, 128n12, 133n52

health, 2, 4, 17, 36, 43, 74, 104, 111n24, 111n25, 111n26, 114n10, 128n12, 131n36, 132n44

holding environment, 28–29, 36

Holy Spirit, 4, 8, 23, 25, 47–52, 56–62, 70, 77, 83–85, 87, 90, 94–95, 97, 100, 102, 104, 105, 111n19, 117n5, 121n39, 123n55, 123n57

hope, 11, 15, 17–18, 23–24, 29, 31, 34, 36, 38–39, 41–42, 57, 61–62, 73–75, 80–83, 88, 96, 99, 109n5, 118n16, 127n29

hospitality, 2, 8–9, 19, 69–70, 93, 98–99

illness, 14, 43

illusion, 29, 31, 120n38, 130n32

image, 14, 23–24, 36, 39–43, 52, 54, 56, 73–76, 91, 93, 108n8, 116n42, 116n45, 116n48, 122n49, 123n55, 124n2

imagination, 11, 40–41, 76, 102, 121n39
imago Dei, 56, 91, 120, 121n49
inclusion, 6, 20, 98
interdependence, 20, 28

Jesus Christ, 62, 90, 113n42, 117n8, 118n10, 128n10; mediator of friendship, 84, 95, 104; revelation of God, 64

kingdom of God, 2, 7, 47, 124n2
koinonia, 95, 102, 133n51

music, 21, 31, 35, 49, 74, 78, 98
mutuality, 3, 21, 38, 56, 58, 77–78, 93, 99, 100, 104

Nirje, Bengt, 12
normalization, 12–13
Nouwen, Henri, 118n16

object-relations psychology, 36

pastoral friendship groups, 100–102, 133n51, 133n52
person-centered support, 8, 9, 11–12, 14–18, 21–35, 27–44, 46, 58–59, 61–62, 64–65, 70, 84–85, 87, 90, 95–97, 99, 100, 104–5, 112n31, 117n4, 124n1, 126n27
play, 25, 27–28, 34–43, 46, 49, 62–65, 67–69, 71, 73–76, 81–84, 91, 96, 115n23
poetry, 34, 59, 73, 76
prayer, 6, 23, 57–59, 89, 98, 101, 133n50; Lord's Prayer, 102
President's Committee on Mental Retardation, 12, 109n4

rationality, 56, 122n53
reason and will, 48, 50, 122n53

religious education, 98

self-discovery, 34, 36, 95, 114n6
shalom, 17, 18, 111n26
shame, 40, 80–83, 118n15
Social Role Valorization, 13
soul: *see* body, and soul
space, 20, 25, 27–31, 34, 36–37, 39–41, 43–44, 46, 49, 56–57, 59, 64, 67–70, 81–83, 94, 96–98, 100, 105, 114n6, 116n40
Sunday school, 18, 87, 98, 103
supportive care group, 19–20, 112n31, 129n21
symbols, 34, 39

Trinity, 24
true self, 24–25, 30–38, 42–43
trust, 9, 23, 25, 31, 35, 37, 81–83, 91, 104, 128n10

vocation, 8, 15–18, 21, 23–25, 28, 43, 45–47, 50, 53, 59, 63, 85, 88–92, 94–95, 101, 104–5, 110n17, 110n18, 111n22, 117n4, 117n8, 118n10, 118n11, 128n12, 130n32, 131n37

welcome, 2, 7, 20, 37, 53, 69–70, 82, 87, 89, 93, 97–98, 100, 103, 105
wholeness, 2, 4, 11, 17, 61
witnesses, 3, 16, 46, 89, 90, 94
witness, 4, 9, 18, 20–21, 28, 41, 59, 87–88, 92–93, 97, 100, 105, 128n11
Wolfensberger, Wolf, 12–13
World Health Organization, 17
worship, 6, 87, 89, 98, 100, 102, 103, 112n37, 119n27, 133n50

OTHER BOOKS IN THE SERIES

The Bible and Disability: A Commentary
Edited by Sarah J. Melcher, Mikeal C. Parsons, and Amos Yong

*Becoming Friends of Time: Disability, Timefullness,
and Gentle Discipleship*
John Swinton

Disability and World Religions: An Introduction
Edited by Darla Y. Schumm and Michael Stoltzfus

Madness: American Protestant Responses to Mental Illness
Heather H. Vacek

Disability, Providence, and Ethics: Bridging Gaps, Transforming Lives
Hans S. Reinders

Flannery O'Connor: Writing a Theology of Disabled Humanity
Timothy J. Basselin

*Theology and Down Syndrome: Reimagining Disability
in Late Modernity*
Amos Yong